FOR THE SAKE OF OUR YOUTH

A Therapist's Perspective
on Raising Your Family
in Today's Culture

• • •

TESSA STUCKEY, M.A.

LICENSED PROFESSIONAL COUNSELOR

RIVER GROVE
BOOKS

This book is intended as a reference volume only. It is sold with the understanding that the publisher and author are not engaged in rendering any professional services. The information given here is designed to help you make informed decisions. If you suspect that you have a problem that might require professional treatment or advice, you should seek competent help.

Published by River Grove Books
Austin, TX
www.rivergrovebooks.com

Distributed by River Grove Books

Design and composition by Greenleaf Book Group and Kim Lance
Cover design by Greenleaf Book Group and Kim Lance

Publisher's Cataloging-in-Publication data is available.

Print ISBN: 978-1-63299-287-1

eBook ISBN: 978-1-63299-288-8

First Edition

To my four boys:

Beau Grayson, Tripp Jameson, Heath River, and Jed August.

May you each feel safe, connected, and valued

as you take on this big world.

Contents

Preface

Being the child of two therapists can make for an interesting upbringing. Hearing "And how did that make you feel?" regularly became an annoyance of mine by the age of 10. There were moments when I blamed my parents' profession for uncomfortable situations and decided at a very young age that I didn't want to continue living in a "therapeutic" lifestyle. I longed to get as far away from the mental health field as possible but still held on to the desire to be a helper in this world. It's funny how life works sometimes.

Friends have always come to me for advice. I have never been sure what attracted them to me in that way, but it always made me feel needed and important, so I was comfortable taking on that role. I would talk them through their crushes or the fights they had with their parents. It was natural for me. I suppose growing up in a house with two psychologists may have had something to do with it; human behavior and mental health were common topics at the dinner table. I was taught to think through typical life situations by setting goals, analyzing, and reflecting on myself.

My calling

When I was a teenager, I didn't feel comfortable talking to my parents. Yep, that's right. Even therapists have teens who don't want to talk to them. Of my siblings, I was the toughest through those years. My independent, adventurous soul mixed with my curious and eager heart created quite the challenge for my parents—from sneaking out from a second-floor window to not showing any interest in school to rolling my eyes and asking "Why!?" through every lecture. I didn't want to hear what they had to say and convinced myself that they had no idea how hard my life was and didn't care. The anger and tension in my relationship with my parents bothered me. Was this inevitable? Was this just the natural parent–teen relationship?

Through the most emotionally confusing season of one's life (the teenage years), I have found that this distance is, in fact, natural and inevitable. As parents, we want our kids to create some gradual distance; that is, we want a healthy distance that prepares them for being independent individuals in this big, scary world. However, many times, when the parent–teenager relationship is filled with anger, tension, and hostility (as my relationship with my parents was), it is unhealthy. Unfortunately, this is extremely common.

As a parent, you can read all the parenting self-help books out there, but unless the advice in those books is realistic about the fact that parents are emotionally attached to their child, all the behavior plans and advice won't make a damn bit of difference. My parents found that to be very true when parenting three teenagers all at once. Here were two professional therapists who specialized in working with people and behaviors, and parenting, at times, still stumped them too.

I made it through those teenage years successfully, as did my parents, and I am now sitting on the other side. I am now a mom *and* a therapist. I have four young boys who teach me new, beautiful things about life every day, but they also drive me to my absolute worst at times. The emotions I experience as a mother are like nothing I have felt before—immense love and fear all at once. It's overwhelming.

Because of my job, I have become familiar with a lot of issues and warning signs that are very helpful to me as a mother. I hear parents complain about their teenagers and teenagers complain about their parents. One thing I've learned that stands out is that parents today are more disconnected from their children than ever before. Our kids are growing up in a world that has become almost impossible for parents to relate to. The needs are the same. The emotions are the same. But the circumstances and influences are very different. That's where I come in. My job has given me an amazing advantage. I get to sit with teenagers, who are currently growing up in this culture, and I listen to their thoughts and their struggles. I hear all of their secrets, their inner thoughts. I am connecting with today's youth, and it is helping me tremendously as a parent.

An epidemic

I had this vision and passion when I decided to become a therapist that I wanted to be a helper for the emotionally confused adolescents of this world. When I started working in private practice and building my clientele, they were mostly female adolescents. I desperately wanted to be their guide and provide a safe place through the toughest years of their life.

When I started, I felt extremely comfortable sitting with these adolescents. I used my own experience as a teen to relate to them, and I was confident that I could help them through school stressors, boyfriend and girlfriend drama, nagging parents, and emotional rollercoasters. But something hit me hard that I wasn't expecting—something that I could not relate to even though I was once from their same hometown and went to the same high school and had strict and "annoying" parents and certainly dealt with my fair share of high school drama. They were thinking about suicide. Some had already attempted suicide. Every single one of my adolescent clients was experiencing suicidal ideation. I became extremely confused, scared, and unqualified.

I was hit hard, not because of suicidal ideation (I expected to face that as a therapist), but most of my clients with suicidal ideation didn't fit what I knew suicidal ideation to look or sound like. I studied suicide in graduate school. I was aware of common causes and how to work with suicidal clients. I had experience working with individuals struggling with suicidal thinking while interning, but this felt different.

These were seemingly normal, typical girls with all the typical teenage issues: boyfriend/girlfriend drama, dating, weed, sex, vaping, bad hair days, insecurities, arguing with mom, being labeled "lazy," grades dropping, dads yelling—all the things we all have heard for years and years and that most of us dealt with at that age as well. But the difference between these girls and me at that age was that their go-to answer was suicide. *All of them* were having suicidal ideation.

The more I listened, the quicker I realized that they didn't have any of those traditional suicidal root causes. Why did suicide seem like a viable solution to them? When I was in high school—which wasn't *that* long ago—the biggest scare for parents was driving accidents. While that is still one of the main concerns for parents, now we need to add teen suicide to that list. What's happening within our youths' hearts and minds that so many of them are suffering so horribly? I know suicide has always been an issue, but what's different now that has made it *the issue*?

The town I work and live in (and also grew up in) was experiencing what is called a *suicide cluster*. That is just what it sounds like: multiple suicides in a short amount of time and typically all done the same way. There had been multiple cases of teenage girls in the area hanging themselves or trying to. I had one young client during this time, while discussing a recent suicide, who said things like, "Well, she was successful; good for her." How can a 14-year-old with a seemingly stable upbringing call suicide a success?

The parents of my clients were coming to me for answers, but I didn't have them. My friends with young children were asking me these questions, and I had nothing to offer them. I absolutely hated that my response was "I don't know."

Raising my four sons in a world where something like this happens is confusing, heartbreaking, and terrifying to me, but suicide now seems to be a common and casual solution for our youth. At the rate we're going, our kids have a 100% chance of knowing multiple kids who take their lives before graduating high school. Let that sink in: the thought of our children having to deal with the grief, heartache, and trauma of knowing someone who has committed suicide. What if your own child has the urge to commit suicide? This is my call to action: to save their lives.

Your children's voice

Typically, therapists have landed this role because they are natural born helpers. And sometimes being a helper blurs together with the passion of wanting to save others. I find myself stuck in that blur often, and my passion drives me to want to save my clients. While being saved is truly a mission that the client can and needs to embark on themselves, because they are the only ones who can truly save themselves, I am fueled by the ambition to do all I can do to provide them with a good setup.

I feel like the biblical Noah building the ark. I know a storm is on its way, and the clouds are ominous, so come with me for protection. I feel like Chicken Little screaming, "The sky is falling! The sky is falling!" but, instead, it's "Our kids are falling! Our kids are falling!" I am not crying wolf here. I know this because the parents whose attention I do grasp agree with me and are overwhelmingly grateful for my willingness to share. I get amazing feedback from these parent conversations and presentations and hear comments like, "Every parent needs to know this." I know this because my colleagues ask me questions, and when I answer, they respond with agreement and understanding. I know this because every human I have spoken to about this in my personal life is encouraging me to keep pushing through the struggle because this is too important to give up on.

I know this because my clients, my adolescent clients that currently struggle with this issue, have 100% agreed with me. They have read my work and have approved my research and findings. I'm coming straight from the source. I am their voice. I am my children's voice. I am *your* children's voice. I am here to tell you what I have learned as a therapist and a mother.

Author's Note

Since I was young, I have always kept a journal. It started as a way to express my feelings that maybe I didn't think others had. My little 6-year-old self would write about the challenges I had in the first grade that now, looking back, seem so miniscule and even cute. As I grew older, I continued to write to express and cope when my emotions were too big to keep inside and when I felt uncomfortable opening up to anyone. Through tough times, I also wrote to observe and document as my attempt to remember the raw emotions I felt at the time. I desperately wanted to hold on to those moments so that when I became older, I wouldn't lose touch with the struggles one experiences and feels during young, adolescent years. There were many entries that I wrote statements similar to "Remember this, Tessa, when you have a teenager!! Remember how you feel and how upset you are!!" or "I never want to be one of those grown-ups who hates kids. Be a good grown-up, Tessa. You're a kid now, so remember this when you get really old and have your own kids."

As I get further and further from my teenage years, I become more and more detached from some of those emotions. I can feel them slipping out of my hands; that's a good thing. I've grown up. However, my emotional maturity can and does disconnect me from some of my young, adolescent clients. Reading my journals from my adolescent years helps me reconnect with my teenage self.

As I periodically go through my entries, I am reminded of moments in my youth that had great impact on my emotional maturity. Through this journey with my clients in recent years, I have fallen into remembering my first encounter with suicide, which happened when I was a young 13-year-old at a new, big school.

I was just beginning eighth grade at the new school. I remember walking down the hall, or, rather, I recall my tiny body being pushed down the crowded hall of junior high with more than 2,000 other students. The anxiety was overwhelming. And it didn't help that I had scoliosis and was trying to hide the back brace I had just gotten fitted for under my clothes. For the first time in my life, I felt shy. I didn't want anyone to know about my back, so I kept quiet and didn't say much. Finally, after a few weeks into the school year, I made a friend, Aubrey. We were in an elective together. It was basically study hall, so we got to gossip, do our makeup, laugh, and hang out for the entire period. It was relieving to have someone to open up to. She was beautiful, friendly, and seemed to know everyone.

We had a notebook that we used to write notes to each other. We decorated the front with flowers and our names in bubble letters, and we would pass it back and forth to each other between classes. I felt important to somebody.

In our notes, we talked about cute boys (or at least that was the majority of my notes to her) and annoying stressors. We discussed what we did over the weekend and our nerves about entering high school. But oftentimes, what she wrote about was very different than what was on my mind. Her daily stressors were different, harder. Aubrey's notes to me were often about being sad about her home life and the divorce of her parents. While I was excited to have a new friend and talk about cute boys, she was sharing darker thoughts and emotions. I longed to help her; though I didn't understand her situation. I just knew I wanted to save her and make her happy.

One afternoon, at the end of the school day, she handed the notebook to me, and I went on my way, knowing I would read what she had written later. Hours later, I opened our notebook. I began feeling uneasy as I read her words, which did not match the cute flowers or colorful pen strokes that filled the pages. I became confused. She wrote about how she wanted to kill herself. She wrote that she was going to do it after school and shared how she would do it. It was a suicide note. And I was reading it hours after she had said she was going to kill herself. I was quickly filled with anxiety, fear, and sadness.

I rushed to my mom after reading her note. I remember I was crying when my mom read it and I was so annoyed that she remained so calm. I remember yelling at her, "We don't have time for you to read it, Mom! We have to go over to her house now!" After she read it, she calmly reached for the house phone. "Tessa, do you have her home phone number?" Why was my mom acting so cool and collected? Why wasn't she freaking out with me? Why weren't we running to the car to rush to her house? (Even though I had no idea where she lived. I didn't even have her phone number.)

Luckily, we knew someone who was friends with her mom, we were able to get her phone number, and my mom called her mom. With urgency and a firm, yet soothing tone, my mom explained to her what we had just read. Her mom didn't seem shocked, but she sounded scared. While still on the phone with my mom, she rushed to Aubrey's locked bedroom door. She got her son to knock down the door and found Aubrey on the floor with blood all over her arms, scissors in her hand, and an empty pill bottle lying next to her. She was unconscious but breathing.

I later learned that they had rushed her to the hospital, and she had to get her stomach pumped and stitches where she'd cut herself. I was so glad she was okay.

What happened with Aubrey is branded in my brain—it was a turning point for me. Looking back at those letters, I realize now that my innocent, young adolescent mind didn't see what was happening. While I was excited to have a new friend and talk about cute boys and "annoying" stuff in our lives, she was going through stuff that was heavier. Stuff at home with her parents' divorce and a heartbreaking home life. I really wanted to help her, even though I didn't fully understand her situation. I just knew I wanted to save her and make her happy.

My little 13-year-old naive self wasn't feeling so innocent or oblivious anymore. I had been introduced to some real, dark aspects of life. Luckily, that day, I didn't have to experience the dark emotion of guilt or secondary trauma.

I never saw Aubrey again. Naturally, we drifted apart after her move to a different town. Aubrey was someone who was suffering internally and needed help. She was probably showing signs of depression, had experienced trauma and abuse, and was struggling every day to make it through.

A few years ago, we became Facebook friends, and I learned that she had gone on to college and had a career, a boyfriend, and a good, happy life—at least that's what I could see through Facebook. Unfortunately, about a year ago, I found out that my sweet friend from the eighth grade took her own life. She had still been miserable. She had still needed help. She had been suffering all along. I hope to help my clients—and to help your children through this book—avoid this kind of lifelong depression.

The Storm

L ife is hard. I know this may seem obvious to some; however, I find that most people keep denying or avoiding the effort needed to feel truly fulfilled. Many times, we're stuck in this place thinking, "Why is *my* life so hard? Why am I the *only one* who has it so hard?" Life is hard for everyone. Life being hard does not always equal life being bad. But whether we do something with life's difficulty to make it good or bad is up to each of us, individually.

Other than being a young kid, I can't think of a time when life was easy. Even then, though having good, interactive parents, I was met with expectations and appropriate challenges for each developmental stage I was in. I bet if you were face-to-face with your 6-year-old self, you'd remember how life wasn't easy, even back then. Life takes effort and strength. If we hold on to the idea that it should be easy, it will most definitely be exhaustingly hard. But if we know there will be moments of distress and heartache, maybe there's the possibility that we won't be stuck in the shocking stage asking, "Why? Oh, God, why?"

I truly believe that the teenage years are the hardest years—especially emotionally. It baffles me that through this time, teenagers and their parents become so distant from each other. These are the years that guidance is needed the most, but it is pushed away like a disease. Many assume this distance is a result of an overly emotional teen, when, in reality, it's both. Distance is caused by both confused teenagers and fearful parents. It's heartbreaking.

I know that parents love their teens. I know that teens love their parents. So why is it that as individuals, we can't seem to connect with the people who love us the most? I know this from my own teenage experience but now as a therapist, I see it daily. Parents are literally given to each of us as guidance counselors and protectors. But the exact opposite often happens.

This is my plea to you for help for all of our children's futures, as well as for our own peace of mind as parents. Every parent's biggest fear is to lose their child to death. That is why we warn them of the negatives in this world. We teach them how to take care of themselves, from wiping their own butt to studying for a chemistry test. We teach them how to be good, defensive drivers and warn them of the consequences of bad choices. We have something on our hands now that I ask you to add to your list. There is a cultural storm that has hit and is wiping out those we love and is pulling more and more down with them: an epidemic of suicide. Our kids are next.

I ask, as you read this book, to open your mind and heart with the desire to show your child how much you care for him or her. People joke all the time, "Oh, if only babies came with a manual, I would know what to do!" Although this isn't necessarily a manual, it can help bring understanding to what is affecting kids and teens today. We can learn what to do as their parents within this modern world. Certainly, it does not hold answers to all situations, but I truly believe that, with what I share with you and your choice to put it into action, it can help tremendously and make parenting easier and maybe even enjoyable!

For those of you who have younger kids, you may not think this applies to you. Surely, your kids are too young to contemplate suicide. But, sadly, it does apply. Who knew that something so serious that teenagers are dealing with is something that we may need to deal with now? I wouldn't have had any idea if it weren't for my job. But one thing I know for sure: If I can put things into action while mine are little to prevent some sorrow while they are adolescents, you bet your bottom dollar I'm going to do it. And I know you feel the same. I can't sit back and allow others to be unaware of what I know. Most of my research and the original purpose of this book was for parents of young kids, such as yourself. I want to get the attention of those who have no idea this would pertain to them. If we don't make some changes now, consider how it will affect your future with your kids.

Our current crisis: Teen suicide

A few short months after starting my private practice, I received a voicemail from a tearful woman. She was calling because she had heard I worked well with teenagers and wanted to get her 16-year-old daughter, Layton, in to see me quickly. I called her back, and when she answered, I could hear her breathing heavily as she struggled to find the strength to talk to me. When she began speaking, her voice trembled. She shared that she was worried her daughter was having suicidal thoughts. *Okay,* I thought, *suicidal thoughts, depressed teen—I've got this. No biggie.* However, I was not prepared for what she told me next. Her 16-year-old daughter, surprisingly, was not the reason for the tears. Just two months prior to this phone call, her youngest daughter, Emily, had unexpectedly ended her own life.

Emily was 15. She was in the ninth grade and involved in many school organizations. She had good friends, a supportive older sister, and parents who were involved in her day-to-day life. Emily's parents fought from time to time, and her mom didn't handle stress very well. Tension was a common vibe in the house. Emily's dad had recently lost his job, and financial stressors were on her parents' minds constantly.

Emily spent most of her time with her mom and sister. She had a good set of friends whom she spent time with during school and sometimes on the weekends. Emily was a happy, typical 15-year-old, or so it seemed.

Looking at Emily's social media accounts, everything seemed fine. The occasional teenage drama overwhelmed her, but what teenage girl doesn't experience drama? Some sibling competition was present, but what sibling doesn't have that? Emily's life was following the typical route that a healthy and stable teenager experiences: some ups, a lot of emotional downs, family conflict, and school stressors mixed with accomplishments in extracurriculars, friendships that were fickle, confusing thoughts of the world that we live in, and smiling pictures flooding her Instagram page.

When her mom found her, just 20 minutes after having a discussion with her downstairs, Emily hadn't lost her life yet. The doctors had hope for her survival. For a solid week, Emily's family lay by her side, being told that there was a 95% chance she would fully recover. Through sleepless nights, taking shifts, endless tears, and desperate prayers, her family held her hand, ready for her to open her eyes again and return to their normal life. Weeks went by, and one morning, the doctor approached the family to share that Emily would, in fact, not recover. Her brain had lost too much oxygen. Her family faced the unimaginable reality that they had lost her forever. Emily's family would never be the same.

I was able to get Layton in for a session the same week I spoke with her mom. Grieving the loss of her sister while juggling everyday life stressors was overwhelming, and her anxiety was taking over. "Why did she do it?" Layton would ask repeatedly. "She was fine. We were fine. We were a normal family! I just don't get it. And now all I want to do is die. I don't want to be here either! Why did she do it?"

Layton found that the only thing keeping her going, the only thing keeping her from ending her *own* life, was the thought of her parents having to grieve the loss of two children. She felt she had to stay strong for her mom when all she felt was weakness. She was hiding the truth; she really wanted end her own life as well. She became consumed with these thoughts and saw no sign of relief. She was tired, and she felt defeated and alone.

Each week, I met with Layton, allowing her to process and talk through what she was feeling. "The only thing I can think of is that I've always been a better athlete. Is that why she did it? Was she jealous? Did I pressure her? Was this my fault?" We discussed what suicidal individuals look like, and I attempted to provide comfort for her by letting her know that it wasn't her fault.

"But that's just the thing. Emily was none of those things. She didn't isolate herself or show a single sign of depression. This doesn't fit Emily, and it makes me mad when everyone says that shit. She wasn't mentally ill! I know my sister. And everything you're saying, was not my sister."

Layton and her mom worked through their grieving with me for almost two years, until they moved away to start a new chapter. Through the work that we did together, we addressed hard moments and emotions, such as guilt and confusion, head-on. I became a punching bag for the anger and defeat that they felt. I held their hands while they relived the last moments of Emily's life in the hospital. They found acceptance with the reality that Emily didn't show any sign of mental illness or suicidal thinking, and I helped them process the shock that hit them hard. We were able to manage Layton's suicidal ideation and figured out where to place that energy, so it became productive rather than destructive.

But I couldn't shake what happened with Emily. I couldn't get Layton's words out of my head. Emily's story is eerily similar to those of many teenagers and young adults throughout the country. They show no signs of despair. They just suddenly take their own lives, leaving no explanation and shaking their families to their core.

Our current crisis: Self-harm

Self-harm is just as prevalent as—if not more so than—suicidal ideation, for all the exact same reasons suicidal ideation is. Self-harm is much more common in girls but is absolutely present for boys as well. It's as if everyone is trying to cope, but because their coping skill is on their smart device, it can only do so much. We haven't prepped anyone for the storm of existing as an adolescent in today's world, and they're stuck in the middle of it.

Skylar was 14. She was in the eighth grade and filled with anxiety over the thought of entering high school. Everything she had heard, mostly from teachers, was horrifying. As a straight-A student in junior high, she was convinced she was going to be a failure in high school.

The first time I met Skylar, I was mesmerized by her natural beauty. She had long, beach-waved hair, beautiful complexion, and piercing eyes. And then she began to talk. What a smart and mature girl! She didn't need any warming up to feel comfortable talking with me. She opened up immediately. She shared about her relationship with her parents and all of the things she was interested in with her friends. She expressed a healthy family life and environment—for the most part, nothing too concerning but certainly not picture perfect. She enjoyed school and was proud of how well she did. She was involved in a school team sport, and although she sometimes found herself getting mixed up in the drama, she had a good handle on her self-awareness to deal with it. She had a good group of friends and felt comfortable within her social world, most of the time.

As she was talking with me one day, she started to express how much she hated herself. She expressed how she had the urge to cut herself and sometimes thought about suicide.

I started asking all the questions I was supposed to. I needed to get an idea of how serious this was. Was it a mental illness or a mental health issue caused by cultural influences?

She revealed that she had cut herself about five times in the past year and shared that, for a few seconds, it helped her feel better.

I asked her what her opinion of cutting was and why people believed it was unhealthy.

She agreed that it wasn't healthy but still found that she wanted to do it and hated that about herself. She was benefiting from it, even if only for a few seconds.

I asked her, "You say you don't want to do it, but I'm not sure if I believe that. It seems more that you *want* to not want to do it."

She said, "YES! THAT'S IT! I want to not want it. Because I think I do, deep down, want it. Especially if I'm having a bad day or there's too much drama going on."

If she hadn't benefited from those five times she'd done it, she wouldn't have imagined doing it again after the first cut.

I asked her whether she could go back into her memory bank and help me understand the beginning thought process for her with cutting and suicidal thinking. I helped her rewind her personal timeline to her first memory of understanding what cutting and suicide was and how she even knew it existed.

Her response was similar to one I hear often: "I remember in the sixth grade having a friend that talked about suicide, and I think I knew about cutting just because of movies and shows and stuff."

There is a strong element of trust that is present within peer relationships whether there is a healthy understanding of the subject or not. Sometimes this is due to pressure, insecurity, or simply feeling close and comfortable with that friend. The moment suicide and self-harm are learned by a young mind from someone who is a peer or close to the same age, it is officially brought to the table. Anything that kids learn from other kids, whether it is accurate or not, has then been absorbed into the brain and is available for exploration and discovery.

The risk of both suicide attempts and suicide is significantly higher in those who have engaged in self-harm. About 70% of those who have engaged in self-harm have attempted suicide at least once.[1] While studying my clients who struggled with self-harm, it was undeniable the similarities with those struggling with suicidal ideation.

The research

The suicide rate for adolescents has risen significantly in the past 10 years.[2] From speaking with mental health professionals, therapists, psychiatrists, and hospitals, locally and across the nation, I know that they are seeing the same things I am seeing in my own office. There have been recent suicide clusters of young teens around the ages of 13–15. Male teens have always had a higher rate, and although that is still the case, the adolescent female suicide rate is aggressively rising. For example, while conducting my own research study and using research from data reports from the Houston morgue, I found that in 2004, there were a total of 65 reported suicides among teen boys in the Houston, Texas area. For girls, there were 16. In 2005, while there were 75 males, there were 29 females. In just one year, it rose 81% for females.[3]

If this follows the trend of other epidemic mental health issues, it will get the attention it needs in 20 or so years when the lawsuits start happening. But I refuse to wait for that to happen. It's like choosing to drink and drive, knowing the possible repercussions and then not taking it seriously until you lose your best friend or hit another car. I will not allow my kids or any others to be the guinea pigs any longer.

---

1   Grandclerc S, De Labrouhe D, Spodenkiewicz M, Lachal J, Moro MR. "Relations between Nonsuicidal Self-Injury and Suicidal Behavior in Adolescence: A Systematic Review." *PLoS One* 11(4), art. e0153760 (2016). https://www.ncbi.nlm.nih.gov/pmc/articles/PMC4835048/

2   Suicide statistics, American Foundation for Suicide Prevention, https://afsp.org/about-suicide/suicide-statistics.

3   Houston area data from interviews with families, teens, and therapists conducted by the author from 2015 to 2018 and from records from Harris County and Montgomery County morgues from 2004 to 2018.

What is happening today with suicide is a crisis. It may not be a crisis for you at this current moment, but it's headed our way whether we choose to face it or not. It is a silent epidemic that isn't going away. Many parents are in denial. Many have no idea how bad it has gotten. And although I work with adolescents and their parents on a daily basis to help them get through this crisis, I can't help but think, "What can I do with my kids *now*, so this isn't in our future?"

A young client of mine said, practically yelling at me, "You need to talk to parents about this! You need to talk to parents of young kids—no, wait. You need to talk to *all* parents about this. I am miserable, and my parents don't believe me. They think I'm being a dramatic teen and don't listen to me. I feel as if I'm losing my mind. Is it supposed to be this miserable? If there was something my parents could have done differently when I was little, I wish they had. I wish I didn't feel this way and that this wasn't happening right now. I want to die."

We need to foster connection

My main focus is on building strong connections with your children to provide protection for your family. I am here as a therapist to share what I have learned. More importantly, as a fellow parent, I feel it is my duty to protect my kids, and I am called to reach out to you so you can protect yours as well.

I am scared, and my honest hope is to scare you a little, to get your attention. I need you to hear me and listen to what I have found. Your children need you to hear this. Join me in understanding the hurt that is happening and in connecting with your children. My goal with this book is to unite parents and teens or future teens, to promote universal love and respect. My ultimate goal is to fight this storm of suicide with confidence and with all the right gear.

During training as a therapist, you are taught that every person who has suicidal thinking has signs of mental illnesses and needs medication to help bring those thoughts to a halt to help make daily struggles manageable. People vulnerable to suicidal ideation have been described as isolated, as feeling they have no hope or are a burden to others. Many mental health professionals have equated these people as struggling with a mental illness, such as depression, anxiety, bipolar disorder, substance abuse, or post-traumatic stress disorder (PTSD) and have pursued a line of treatment appropriate for those with mental illness. This is how mental health professionals have been taught throughout the years.

Until now, there has been no cause for reevaluation or shift in this training and understanding of suicidality. Today, there is a caveat, though. A distinction needs to be made between those with mental illness and those with suicidal ideation. They are not necessarily one and the same anymore.

A cultural wave has caused this rise in suicidal rates and suicidal ideation among young adults and teenagers. By continuing to treat individuals struggling with suicidal thoughts who may not have a mental illness or fall into the original understanding of suicidality as if they have a mental illness, we aren't addressing the right issues and could potentially be causing more harm than good.

Many people ask why everyone is so depressed and anxious? What does everyone have to be so upset about? After all, life today is in many ways far "easier" than it was in previous eras, right? But struggle is relative. What one feels is the "worst thing ever," might look pretty good to someone else.

Although most of us aren't fighting to stay alive from outside predators, we now have to fight to stay alive with our own internal predators: self-loathing, depression, anxiety, obsessive thoughts, and self-shaming. They've become overwhelming and are seemingly impossible to fight for youth today. Now add to those predators the cultural trends of suicide becoming a viable option to escape overwhelming stress, the constant need for immediate gratification, the lack of personal connection, not feeling truly seen or heard, the monumental influence of social media, and the often-underestimated amount of pressure facing teens today. These six pressing cultural influences have led to the rise in suicide rates. We'll spend the first part of the book discussing them and then will tackle what to do about them. Let's get to it.

PART 1

Six Cultural Influences Affecting Youth Today

have found six cultural influences affecting youth today that have contributed to the rise in depression, anxiety, suicidal ideation, and self-harm. These influences work together to create a scary situation many young adults and adolescents are currently facing. In mental health, many factors mesh together, blur together, and affect one another. Although I have done my best to separate these factors, many are unavoidably connected. Here, you will gain understanding of what each influence is. My hope is that if we can understand these influences better, perhaps, as parents, we will be better able to help our children navigate these dark waters. Let's not waste any more time.

A Glorified Option

"I am so exhausted. We have been to four hospitals in the past three years, and I don't think I've gotten any sleep since it all began. I just want her to be okay. I want to know that she isn't going to try it again. I want to live the life that others are living with their kids. How have we gotten here?"

—MOTHER OF A 15-YEAR-OLD STRUGGLING WITH SUICIDAL IDEATION AND SELF-HARM

t was a normal Monday when I got to work. I had about seven adolescent clients on my schedule for the day. I began seeing them, one by one, and I realized it wasn't a normal day at all. Every one of these youths was having thoughts of suicide. This is how the conversation went with almost all of them:

I asked, "So what'd you do this weekend? Watch anything good?"

My clients responded with something like, "Yes! I binge-watched a show about teen suicide."

"Oh!" I said, "I haven't heard of that. Tell me about it."

"It's about this girl who commits suicide and how the town reacts to it. It shows all the stuff she went through leading up to it and then shows her doing it. It was so good; you have to watch it."

"Hmm, okay." I said. "I'll have to check it out. It sounds pretty graphic. Can we talk about how it was for you to watch that?"

"Yeah, it was really hard actually."

At first, I thought it was just a local problem. But once I realized how many shows and movies deal with teen suicide—and the number seems to be growing—I quickly saw that this was much bigger than our local town. I watched several of them, and although they were compelling, they got my attention in a different way. As I watched them, it was very easy to get engulfed in the story lines, but I couldn't help but think, "This is disturbing for me, and I don't have any suicidal ideation. What is this doing to those who do?" I did have one client who admitted she had to turn off a particular show because it was too "triggering" for her. Although the intentions of these shows and movies may be benign, they may, at best, indicate a wider trend of teen suicide, and, at worst, they may contribute to a social trend of romanticizing or normalizing it.

Suicide is romanticized

Many TV shows and movies exaggerate to create a gripping story line, and many times, it sets the tone for the viewers' expectations. Movies and shows that romanticize and glorify suicide create a fantasy that the person who is now dead gets to experience everyone missing him or her. It feels as though the main character is with you throughout the whole story, even though they are dead.

Young minds are impressionable. While they are figuring out their world and how to shape their identity, they easily hold on to ideas in order to create their narrative as an individual. Many teenagers have a hard time grasping the finality and severity of suicide but, rather, are enamored with the glorified outcome that is displayed in media depictions of it. I haven't yet seen a show or movie where someone commits suicide and the screen goes black—end of the show.

In therapy, we talk a lot about events that have significant weight in a client's life story and the emotional impact of such events. Many times, they are traumatic; sometimes, they are motivating. Most certainly, the client will experience some level of an emotional takeaway or trauma.

Suicide is normalized

Today, suicide seems to be talked about more than it ever has been. With the increased rate of suicide nationwide, it seems only natural to react with the daunting topic present in conversations and thoughts. When a community experiences a very young adolescent, as young as 10 or 12, ending their life, it sends everyone into a state of confusion, shock, and panic. How can they *not* talk about it? Sometimes talking about it feels like the *only* thing one can do.

When we talk about a topic over and over and over again, it becomes something that is on our mind. And the more it is being talked about, the easier it is for us to become desensitized to the idea of it.

When someone is involved in any sort of traumatic event or a close call, people talk. So it is only natural that most of the community will be talking about high school students who are committing or attempting suicide. Therefore, friends of these students, family members, teachers, principals, churches, organizations, and schools in surrounding areas will all talk about it. And if it's on the forefront of their mind—especially an adolescent's young mind—it may become a credible solution to their own problems.

The domino effect

Emotional trauma is something I was able to avoid when a childhood friend tried to commit suicide when we were in the eighth grade. I can't imagine how I would have reacted or handled it if the suicide attempt had become a completion. My guess is *not well*. You don't know how you will be affected by any emotional trauma, not to mention suicide. Now imagine (or maybe you don't have to even imagine; maybe you know this all too well) a teenager whose sister or friend just attempted or committed suicide. Teenagers are already going through enough emotional ups and downs. And then you add that emotional trauma? Talk about depression. Talk about confusion. Talk about loneliness and existential questioning. Once suicide is an option for one young mind, it is likely to become an option for another. It's officially on the table.

Those who have been affected by suicide in any way are speaking out. There is a pull to spread awareness and share difficult stories. The intention to put this to a stop is strong. The desire to let others know that it's okay to not be okay is the new perspective on mental illnesses. This is wonderful and groundbreaking. However, if it is not balanced with the appropriate preventative care, we are only contributing to the domino effect. Adolescents' brains are still developing, and since they are so impressionable, their takeaway of the awareness stories is, many times, not the one intended for positive production.

The adolescent brain

It's not entirely teenagers' fault that they act out. The prefrontal cortex is one of the last areas of the brain to develop, and it happens to be the center of cognitive thinking. That includes your ability to have good judgment and decision-making, the ability to control your emotions and be self-aware, control impulses and risk-taking, and to consider long-term consequences. The prefrontal cortex isn't fully developed until we reach ages 25–28. Now the choices we all made in high school—and even college—might make more sense. I'm not necessarily here to make excuses for bad behavior, but, as parents, if we can remember the fact that our children's brains are still developing, it might help with some future situations and discussions.

Let's add this up: A lack of cognitive thinking added to emotional trauma, with suicide as an option, and on top of all that, teenage hormones . . . This is a scary formula. The social trend of suicide being more common and more of a seemingly viable option for teen problems helps create a dangerous situation. But we can address that danger with preventative care.

2

Immediate Gratification

"He has lived a good life. We have had a stable and healthy family. He was always such a happy boy. Why would he talk about suicide? What are we missing here?"

—MOTHER OF A 16-YEAR-OLD WITH NO PREVIOUS MENTAL ILLNESS SYMPTOMS

Leigha was on her fifth high school by her junior year. She kept switching schools to better her social situation and mental state. Her first was a public school, and there were girls who were mean to her. I never got the full story but from what I understood, she was being bullied. So her parents sought out a different school for her. During the few months at that first high school, she became suicidal and practiced self-harm.

Leigha's second high school was another public school in the district. She had been approved for transfer and after about three months of attendance, she started to experience similar problems. When spending time with her and talking through her thoughts, she shared experiences of getting close to friends in a short period of time and then scaring them away. She would give her all to these friends, but it wasn't reciprocated, and she would give up and move on. During those three months at that school, she had six "best friends" whom she described more like sisters, but none of those friendships lasted long.

Leigha's third high school was a small Christian private school. She got kicked out for partying with some fellow classmates and exploring her sexuality with one of them. (He was expelled as well.) She was humiliated, and all of her new best friends turned on her in a heartbeat. I never heard that whole story either. She was at that school for five weeks.

Leigha's fourth high school was another private Christian school. She was there for almost eight whole months before experiencing similar friend drama. No one liked her. Her reputation was destroyed. She felt lonely and desperate. One evening with me, she spent the whole hour crying because, she said, I was her only friend.

This was a clear pattern. She wasn't connecting well with others, maybe rushed into the relationships and wasn't satisfied when the other person didn't reciprocate as strongly. She experienced some typical life stressors and couldn't bear the discomfort through them. Her suicidal ideation was getting stronger, and we needed to find solutions quick.

She finally landed on her fifth school, another small private school, but this time she went in with some new perspectives and a bit of an emotional protection built up. While she was sharing her comfort at the new school with me, she still showed cause for concern.

One day, she said, "I just can't be happy. Nothing will do the trick. I've been on medication for years. I have tried making new friends. Things with my parents are fine right now. Can't something just make me feel better now? Everything else in this world is instant! Why can't this be fixed instantly too? Killing myself is the only way for me to stop feeling this *now*."

We want it now!

Many of us have become impatient individuals today. Admit it; you're included in this. Everything is too convenient and available literally right in our hands. Waiting for someone to respond to a text has become torture.

Waiting for the next episode of your favorite show seems impossible, so you binge the whole season.

The difference between my client and me is that I didn't go through my teenage years or upbringing with such instant gratification. Yes, I had it easier than previous generations; I had my first email account at 11. Today's lifestyle contributes to this instant gratification problem in ways that you wouldn't even believe.

Growing up, my Fridays were reserved for family movie night. Every Friday, we would leave the house, get in a car, go to the local Blockbuster or Take One Video, and strolled the aisles for a good bit of time. We would check out the newest movies, but since there were only two copies of those, we were usually left looking at older options. After debating and the occasional argument over which movie to get, we would settle on one or two and head back home. We would each find our spot on the couch or floor, snuggle up with blankets, and my dad would pop the VHS tape into the VCR. Sometimes, people weren't kind and didn't rewind, so we would have to wait the minute and a half it took to get back to the beginning of the tape. We would then begin the movie, which started with seemingly endless FBI warnings and four or so previews before we finally got to enjoy the flick. That is if we didn't have to pause the movie for someone to use the restroom or pop some popcorn.

This whole process was normal to us, and although we would be excited to see a new movie, none of it felt as if it was taking "forever." If kids want to rent a movie today, they don't have to wait for their mom to drive them to Blockbuster on Friday to hope that one of the two copies is there and then go back home and hope that the previous renters had been kind enough to rewind. It takes maybe under a minute to rent a movie for my kids on Apple TV, depending on how fast I can put in the password. What used to take considerable time now takes seconds.

Remember how long it took to see a photograph you took? First, you had to finish a roll of film. That could take months if you were frugal. After it was done, you'd wait for your mom to drive you to the drugstore to drop it off to be developed. Then you'd go back home to wait for the phone call that your photos were ready, usually the next day or two. You would then need your mom to take you back to the drugstore so you could pick up your pictures. Then you would have to wait until the next school day to show them to your friends. That whole process now takes 15 seconds or so, depending on how many pictures you take and what app you're using to edit it.

Almost everything in today's daily life is instant. On the surface, this seems nice, easy, and convenient, but it also causes emotional instability and the inability to build resilience for people (your kids) who don't know anything different. We're depriving our kids of knowing what delayed gratification looks like.

I'll never forget sitting with Leigha discussing her situation. We explored many perspectives and thoughts on suicide and what she thought was causing it to be so common. She looked at me straight in the eye and said, "You've got to be kidding. You don't know? It's simple, Tessa. I want everything, and I want it now."

Technology is a blessing and a curse

Technology is a wonderful tool. It has literally saved lives and has made things much easier and quicker. But it has created a world of imbalance. No one could have predicted the emotional instability this would cause. When a teenager is having a bad day, hormones are strong, suicide is on the table, and they want instant relief. What do they turn to? Strong suicidal ideation seemingly offers them an immediate and permanent fix. They don't have to be diagnosed with depression or anxiety or any other mental health issue, they don't have to spend years on medication to find the right balance of chemicals, and they don't have to spend years building confidence; they can just opt out. They are living in this world that almost seems to be encouraging it, right?

Luckily, anyone born before around 1995 knows a world without this stuff. I was born in the late '80s, so I certainly have had things quicker than others, but I had to learn delayed gratification too. I had pen pals (the best feeling ever was getting a letter in the mail!) and had to wait for phone calls—on a phone connected to the wall in my house. Nothing was available at the click of a button during my upbringing. That's what makes us different from our children. Our prefrontal cortex developed before all this immediate input, so we are able to control our impulses when we have a bad day even within today's culture.

How do we teach our kids that there is no instant fix for some of life's stressors? How do we help them build that patience and emotional strength to get through something really hard and heartbreaking? How do we teach them to have hope and positivity within even in their darkest and lowest moments?

The lack of development of their prefrontal cortex, the hormones coursing through their confused bodies, and the distance between them and you make your child vulnerable to all of the usual stressors. But add to that the seeming viability of suicide and the need for an immediate fix, and your children may embrace suicidal ideation. One way to reduce the immediate fix part of this equation is to teach your children delayed gratification and how to cope properly with all the daily stress and social conflicts of adolescence.

A Lack of Personal Connection

> *"I keep picturing her hanging there, her lifeless body. We had gotten in a fight that afternoon, nothing big, just about her grades. I remember she muttered something going upstairs, but because I was exhausted and angry with her attitude, I didn't respond. I found her the following morning. No one would have guessed she was thinking of this or that she even knew how to do it."*
>
> **—MOTHER OF A 14-YEAR-OLD SUICIDE VICTIM**

magine you are a new mom. You've been feeding, wiping, and burping nonstop. Your spouse comes home and gives you a long look. You're still in your pajamas from last night, your hair is a mess, and there are countless stains on your shirt. He announces he wants to get you out of the house and suggests your little family go out to dinner. You quickly make yourself somewhat presentable, grab the diaper bag, and head out. After the first two minutes of sitting at the table, your sweet baby starts to fuss. Anxiety hits as you don't want your one outing to be ruined with cries, but you also don't want others to be bothered or to stare at you.

One of the "joys" of becoming a new mom is not knowing what the hell to do when your baby starts to fuss. Maybe he's tired. Maybe he has a wet diaper. Maybe his foot is caught in the highchair. Maybe he's hungry. Whatever it is, it becomes a guessing game. But you then remember that a friend tried something with her baby that worked perfectly. It works like a charm *every time*. It'll calm the fussiness and create an atmosphere that's enjoyable for Mom, Dad, and the rest of the restaurant.

You pick up your phone and find Netflix and pick Little Einsteins. When you prop that phone up in front of the baby, he instantly stops fussing. He's now completely distracted and enthralled by music and cartoons, and you can go back to enjoying your dinner. It feels like a miracle.

Disconnection starts early

As easy and wonderful as it seems, in that moment, acting out of desperation, you created a disconnection between your baby and the world. You chose to distract the baby rather than soothe him. I'm guilty of this as well. Before I started my research, it was *much* easier to prop my child in front of a phone. I would ignore what was actually bothering my baby and choose to mask it with Netflix or some silly video of a monkey beating on drums instead. For some, this may sound dramatic. But look around. What do you see when you go out to eat? I see families who aren't talking. I see families who are all separately on their phones, playing games, checking stats, replying to emails, checking Instagram—zero personal connection.

And it begins as early as when your baby is a few months old. Not only are you disconnecting your child from the table, but you've just created an expectation, a new habit. Every time you go out to eat, your child will expect that same distraction. And if he doesn't get it, he will fuss until he does. He won't learn how to sit in a restaurant without it. So you justify it by telling yourself, "Oh, I only give him the phone when we go out to eat while he's little. It won't be like this forever." So when *do* you stop it? When he's 3 and throwing himself on the floor kicking and screaming? When he's 7 and starts to whine about playing games while waiting for his mac 'n' cheese? It's not pleasant going out to eat with a bunch of fuss buckets, is it? So many of us have eliminated the fuss by providing an easy solution, a Band-Aid. But it's part of the problem. It's a *big* part of the problem.

Personal connections are important

Loneliness is intense and consuming. It can become so overwhelming that your judgment is clouded, whether your prefrontal cortex is developed or not. I've felt it. I've acted out in ways that I am not proud of due to it, and I know many others who have as well. The human race has never been so lonely. Communities are not being formed or encouraged. Tribes are not being established or sought. Connections are not being made.

As humans, it is in our DNA to long for companions, attachments, and connections. Studies have shown the effects of babies in orphanages that are not touched or held; some have died due to this deprivation.[4] What happens when we believe that we don't belong or are not accepted or lack a support system? Loneliness. Depression. Self-loathing. We don't actually experience true connection, not true personal connection anyway. And it's not happening only with youth; it's adults too. This can't be news to you.

I was taking my son to karate one day. As we waited in the hallway, I noticed my son, his brothers, and I were the only ones talking. Everyone else was very quiet. How was it possible that a hallway full of young boys was quiet? I looked around; every one of those kids was looking down at a screen. I know that peace and quiet is nice; there's no denying that. But when

---

4   "US Experiment on infants withholding affection," St. Paul's Collegiate School Hamilton, blog, https://stpauls. vxcommunity.com/Issue/us-experiment-on-infants-withholding-affection/13213.

will our kids connect if not in the hallway before a karate class? During school? Nope. School today is focused on academics more than ever and not on social relationships. Maybe during recess? For 30 minutes per day, they get to play and run around with their friends. That just isn't enough.

Social media has created a culture where we no longer need to catch up with anyone. I know exactly what my friends whom I haven't seen in a while have been up to because they post about it. And while I love seeing this, it takes away some of the novelty effect and excitement to see them and spend time with them. We have to search for things to talk about instead of relying on "Tell me what you've been up to!" Personal connection is hard all around, not just for today's youth.

Without the opportunity of interacting and properly connecting with loved ones at a young age, kids today have much more difficulty building the social skills that are necessary in order to get through the day with some comfort and confidence. School days can be daunting, jobs can be overwhelming, events and large gatherings can be uncomfortable—even *with* good social skills. Today, teens and young adults are struggling with social anxiety, which makes it unbearable to be around others. I've noticed within my work and speaking with fellow mental health professionals that social anxiety has become a common concern for adolescents and young adults today. It has amplified as a result of the lack of personal connections being made and the inability to build the social skills needed to comfortably get through a typical, routine day.

Disconnection leads to social anxiety

Social anxiety goes beyond being an introvert, which is the term my clients like to use when trying to describe what they like to do on the weekends and what their social life looks like. Introverts do not always have social anxiety, and those who suffer from social anxiety are not always introverts—at least in the sense that they are not energized by turning inward and spending time to themselves. Those who suffer from social anxiety have perfected the act of avoidance. While consulting with colleagues, I'm hearing more and more cases of young adults and teenagers unable to hold a job or even get a job because they don't want to use the phone or have an anxiety attack from the thought of talking to people. Many teenagers today have no desire to even get their driver's license because they don't want to leave the house. Because we are pro-grammed to connect with others, individuals can easily fall into a very dark depression with very dark thoughts of self-loathing and can have a high risk of suicidal ideation.

Sydney, a sophomore in high school, would come and cry in my office, talking about how she had no one to sit with at lunch. We talked through ways to be approachable and how to talk to others who might be feeling that same loneliness and fear during lunch. I found myself filling up with tears as she sat there expressing how hard it was. I think most of us can identify with that emotion from some point in our lives, and I think we can all agree what a horrible feeling it is.

During one session, I found myself throwing all of my therapeutic techniques out the window and sitting beside her as just another person experiencing that pain with her. Sometimes, as a therapist, this is the most therapeutic thing I can give to my young clients, to let them know that, at least in my office, they aren't alone.

I did offer to come sit with her during lunch. Her initial reaction was "Oh, I wish you could!" but then she followed it with, "Wait, no. That might be embarrassing." She remembered that I was not a student or young enough to pass as one, and she made the right decision to find another solution.

One thing that contributed to Sydney's heightened anxiety, especially at school, was an incident she experienced while playing her school sport during her freshman year. One day, about a year before she started coming to me, she fell badly and got a horrible concussion. She had to have physical therapy to help her get back to her daily routine. Well, coincidentally, another girl on her team experienced a concussion around the same time, except this girl didn't need physical therapy and was back to her usual self the next day. Because of this comparison, the girls on the team, who were Sydney's closest friends, decided that she was faking the severity of her concussion and began making comments that were not very friendly. While Sydney was struggling with her balance and equilibrium, the girls, the ones she felt were her "friends," would sometimes shove her into the wall between classes.

Due to the concussion and doctor's orders, she had to stop playing the sport, therefore creating natural distance between her and these girls. They quickly decided that she was no longer accepted among their group, and Sydney was basically booted out. As teenagers, one of the most important elements throughout those years is to be accepted and liked. And that's the exact opposite of what Sydney was feeling.

Christmas break arrived, and Sydney's brother was home from college. I saw a light in Sydney that I hadn't seen in a while. She was coming to my office with a smile and energy, and "nothing's bugging me lately" was the statement every week that started the hour. She expressed how she had been spending a majority of her break with her older brother. They were bonding and connecting over a show, her artwork, video games, and memes. She felt connected to him.

I immediately got nervous. He was only home for three weeks and would soon be returning to school. She was now dependent solely on her immediate family for connections and socializing. Every time I brought up her brother going back to school, her face would get red, and her chin would begin to quiver. My goal was to help strengthen her emotions, so she was prepped for when he left. She wasn't having it.

Many sessions were spent with Sydney getting upset with me when I would bring up the reality of her brother returning to school. During one intense session, she admitted that she longs to connect with others but felt nobody wanted to connect with her.

Sure enough, the Christmas break came to a close, and Sydney was facing the start of school again, not having any friends to connect with and her brother having returned to school. She expressed the urge to cut, and there were a few scary weeks of strong suicidal thinking that put me and her parents on high alert.

During one session, about a week after her brother had moved back to college, Sydney came in dressed up and with a smile on her face. We began as we usually did, with me asking how she had been since our last session. And then she began to speak, this time not sounding like her normal self but rather using a British accent. She proclaimed, "I've always wanted to be an actress, and therefore, I will begin acting classes next Monday!"

I was taken aback for a quick moment but rather than come across as shocked, I was fueled by her energy and wanted to remind her that I was with her on this journey. Now, this was right up my alley. I too grew up interested in theater. In fact, my sister and I spent a majority of our upbringing practicing different accents while having casual conversations. I decided to pull out some of my old skills and continued our conversation with the best British accent I could muster up.

Sydney was impressed with my casual transition to this accent and felt comfortable carrying on the conversation. "I know that I'm not very good at it, but I am working on it. So much so that I've begun going out to eat using this accent to see how believable I am."

It may have turned into one of the most beneficial sessions I had with Sydney. I would ask her how she was feeling with her thoughts of self-harm, suicide, and about her brother moving back to school. She was open and honest throughout the entirety of the session, using her British accent, of course. With the occasional break in character to giggle and feel silly, it was the perfect balance of deep and authentic yet humorous conversation in order for it to progress smoothly.

Sydney began acting classes, found a sense of passion and connection, and has been thriving since. With a few bumps in the road, Sydney powered through one of the darkest times of her life to find a place of comfort, distraction, and purpose. She made friends, had something to look forward to, and kept busy outside of school and home life.

Attention Seeking

"I can't even get upset with him because I'm fearful he's going to threaten suicide. I know I'm not supposed to dismiss him using suicide as a defense, but, gosh, it is so hard when he uses it every time he's in trouble or I ask him to do something. What am I supposed to do? We know he's just doing it for attention! It's not real!"

—PARENT OF A 16-YEAR-OLD WITH SUICIDAL IDEATION

t is human nature to seek attention. From a very young age, humans practice the act of seeking attention. As babies, we cried to get our parents' attention, so we could be fed or changed or held. But there are negative connotations to wanting attention. We've heard statements such as, "Ugh! He's just doing that for attention!" Most likely, we have said something similar a time or two in our life. Why is there such a negative tone associated with needing attention? If attention is sought through negative behavior, it will have a negative reaction. Parents become annoyed, siblings or friends become jealous and resentful, and adults want to be left alone to focus on their own stressors.

What if we replace the phrase *seeking attention* with *feeling important and valued*? Let's do that: "Ugh! He's just doing that to feel important! He's just doing that to feel valued in this world!" Doesn't sound like such a bad thing to want, right? It is natural to want to feel important. It is natural to want to feel valued. We do things to feel important because maybe we aren't feeling important in that moment or in that season of life. Somehow that very negative statement about wanting attention that helps us minimize someone's emotions has now turned into an emotional, hurting statement that might actually get us to *pay attention.*

Now, I've been told from time to time, especially in my youth, that I have a tendency to maybe sometimes possibly be a tad dramatic. I also look back at my teenage years, read my journals, and see my *huge* longing for attention. Sometimes, I practiced seeking attention in a healthy way, but most of the time, I practiced the search unhealthily.

Research shows that negative emotions are stronger than positive ones.[5] When teenagers experience a negative emotion, I imagine a thick cloud creeps into their brain that alters their judgment (on top of the undeveloped prefrontal cortex that already impairs adolescent decision-making). This helps us understand why someone might seek attention in an unhealthy manner. Typically, positive behavior doesn't receive the same amount of attention as negative behavior. Many times, positive behavior, because it is usually expected, won't get any recognition at all. When I look back and remember the ridiculous decisions I made, purely for attention, I want to cringe.

As parents, we see our kids from young ages acting out for attention. It can get frustrating and can become troubling when your child says or does something unhealthy to seek attention. My thinking road map, I suppose because of my job, is to find understanding and to determine why: Why are so many teenagers coming to me expressing suicidal thoughts

---

5   Aaron Ben-Zeév. "Are Negative Emotions More Important than Positive Emotions?" Psychology Today. July 18, 2010. https://www.psychologytoday.com/us/blog/in-the-name-love/201007/are-negative-emotions-more-important-positive-emotions.

about something I would consider a typical life hardship, such as their mom getting mad about a messy room? Is this the longing to feel important and valued? Why does it feel as if something has changed for teenagers today that is very different from my own teenage experience?

As much as I sought attention, and as dramatic as some may have described me to be, I never would have said I was suicidal if I wasn't truly suicidal. I never would have felt comfortable to lead those who loved me to believe that I was thinking of killing myself. Even as a dramatic, attention-seeking teen, that was going too far for me. I know from speaking with colleagues, teachers, and school counselors, reaching out to mental health professionals nationwide, and talking with parents and teens in my community that something has changed. So what is it? Why has it become a "normal" attention-seeking outlet? It's not a healthy one, but after dozens of conversations with my teenage clients and observing their conversation in my support group, it has become a casual, common choice.

So why are more and more adolescents seeking this feeling of importance and value? What has made these necessary emotions harder to feel?

Let's go back to the year 2000. Think about what you were doing in 2000. Maybe you were in high school. Maybe you were in college. Maybe you were building a family. Imagine a good friend calls you and asks for you to go to www.aboutme.com, and after you wait and wait and wait for the dial-up modem to scream–beep–scream its way to a connection, the site finally pops up. This bright screen with pictures of your friend is huge in front of your face. And then you notice that all of the pictures, and actually the whole site, is all about your friend. It's a bunch of selfies—although that was not a term yet—and a description of who she is and what she likes to do. Now, remember, you're still thinking like your Y2K self. I know, for me, I'd think "What the hell is this? Get over yourself! Why are you showing me a site of stuff just about you? I already know all of this stuff about you and talk to you every day." I don't think I would say it quite as bluntly, but I would certainly be thinking it.

What was unusual in 2000 is today's world of social media, and our kids don't know a world without it. Our world has morphed into a self-absorbed atmosphere that is completely acceptable and expected. The fact that the word *selfie* is now included in *The Merriam-Webster Dictionary* says a lot. This hyperpersonal and self-centered display is now our typical connection with one another, our new normal.

If everyone is self-absorbed, how can anyone feel important? If everyone is hyperfocused on making themselves feel important by looking inward, no one is capable of actually experiencing attention from anybody else. Craving attention has always been around. Parents who are busy have always been around. Because of the culture that we live in today, attention is simply harder to achieve. There's an imbalance.

At a certain age, individuals seek approval and feelings of importance from others outside of their immediate family. Mom and Dad aren't enough anymore. Aunt Jenny raving about how you're going to be a doctor one day doesn't do it. Seeking approval and acceptance in other groups is natural and healthy. Kids start to seek approval from teachers. Adolescents want approval from friends, peers, and coaches. Individuals realize that there is a world outside of the family, and that world has opinions too. These moments help define who this individual believes themselves to be.

Victim mentality

The more I learned about our new cultural longing for attention, the more I discovered something unnerving. I chose to immerse myself into the social media world the way my teen clients have described to me. I began to constantly post to my Snapchat and Instagram stories and published posts daily. It became exhausting and easily took over my way of thinking.

While I was attempting to become noticed on these social media platforms for my digital identity to grow, I felt the power of victim mentality.

Just as I fell into some unhealthy means of seeking attention when I was a teen, a victim mentality has become a top option for many today. The thought, "Maybe if I can get some people to see how hard my life is, I can get the support I need and feel loved," has unfortunately become the go-to solution, except now it is done publicly. Not only are individuals on social media longing for attention because they aren't truly connecting, but they are now finding out that a quick, surefire way to get it is to take on the role of victim every chance they get.

Let me clarify. Taking on that role isn't necessarily new. I can say with confidence that I have played it before, and I'm quite certain you have too. It's a form of hurt (and if we're being truthful here, it's also a form of manipulation) that can be a slippery slope, and sometimes we don't even realize we're doing it. What is different now is that it is public. Many of my clients have admitted to turning to Twitter, Tumblr, Instagram, and Snapchat to vent or seek attention while attempting to cope with a stressful or heartbreaking moment. They have all openly expressed regret and shame linked with the act of doing so on social media, but the reality is that it did validate their longing for feeling important.

I found that most of the Instagram accounts that have a strong following, with the exception of celebrities, created that following by expressing their hardships. Of course, this is not the case for every account with a large following. However, if you are immersed in the social media world much at all, you will notice the attraction to those expressing their personal trauma is higher.

Hardships and true authentic pain are very relatable. While many are sharing their "perfect" life via social media, some are comfortable sharing some true hard times they are facing. It can be very helpful for followers to know that they are not alone and that they are looking up to someone who is being real, authentic, and open about their hardships. This can be beneficial for many. However, when influencers use it as their main attraction for followers, it becomes an influencer not for healing but rather staying in the "feel bad for me" mindset. Surely, their intentions are to share the healing process, but what seems to be happening under the surface is enticing the world of "woe is me" and then creating a more challenging competition for attention. It doesn't necessarily have to be an influencer; if the majority of someone's feed is filled with these messages of pain, it is going to have an influencing effect on the person seeing it day in and day out. We are strongly affected by our surroundings, whether it be our digital surroundings or our physical environment. Hurt people hurt people, even unintentionally.

As I mentioned before, teenagers are impressionable, are emotionally confused, and long to understand their autonomy. I am seeing more and more young individuals exaggerate or glorify their hardships to achieve recognition. Again, this is not to say that there aren't hardships. However, this is feeding into the cultural influence of needing attention much more than ever before. If an adolescent is affected by these cultural influencers, not mental health, and is crying for attention, there is a strong chance they will go to the same extreme to seek help with their strong, dark emotions of hurt.

Of course, we must take it seriously and trust that whoever threatens suicide is truly thinking of suicide. Maybe there isn't a strong plan of action, but the fact that they are saying it means that it's at least on their mind. Either way, it is a cry for attention. How someone asks for attention is important. Remember, it's natural to want to feel important and heard.

Take Jess, for instance, who was going through a lot. She didn't find much interest in school. Her parents didn't like that, so they put a lot of restrictions on her socially. She had a phone, but she wasn't allowed to use apps, and her access to the Internet was restricted. She didn't have much of a social life as it was anyway. She was involved a bit in the school band, so she had some friends there, but she wasn't close to anyone outside of school. At the age of 13, Jess found herself with mixed emotions toward her family and about herself. She found that she was annoyed with her parents almost 100% of the time. She shared that she couldn't recall any recent times of feeling happiness and truly believed that her parents didn't love her and favored her siblings.

Sounds like depression, right? Or hormones? Maybe it's some new emotions that she just hasn't gotten used to? All of these are extremely common problems for the age—that kind of "Woe is me! Please look at me, but don't look at me!" mix of emotions. They want acceptance and love but don't find comfort in what is available or offered. Jess suffered from a mixture of hormones and mild depression.

Jess reported a few thoughts of self-harm and suicidal ideation one time but followed with statements that did not trigger my alarms. Let me be clear about something. It is not that I don't take it seriously. Typically, the mention of suicide calls for serious action and admission to a psychiatric hospital. But I just choose to go a different route for many of my clients—especially if a client doesn't fit into the "traditional" definitions of suicidal.

After a follow-up with her parents, we had a safety plan set in place, and Jess went back to regular weekly visits with me, sharing her emotional rollercoaster. I found numerous times when she would make a pretty dark and serious statement but then contradict that statement 30 seconds later.

"I'm alone in this world. Nobody likes me and I have no friends . . . My best friend, we have three classes together. She is so funny and made me laugh so hard today that I spit out my water. And then one of my other friends who was sitting behind me started snorting, and this guy started making fun of us, but we didn't care because we were having such a good time."

At this point, I'm confused. She literally just said she had no friends and nobody likes her but is now talking about two good friends who made her laugh today. When I confronted her about my confusion, she quickly slumped back down into her chair and replied with, "Yeah, but they don't really count. My mom got so mad at me today because I didn't want to do my homework. I was even crying, and she didn't even care."

Is this possibly an example of the way that teenagers communicate? They want to be taken seriously but, at the same time, make comments similar to "I didn't really mean it." Is it possible to decode this language or teach them that some comments scare us and that we can't help but take them seriously? How do we differentiate between a run-of-the-mill cry for attention and a dangerous one?

It would be very easy for me to roll my eyes and think she's a drama queen, but what good does that do? It completely dismisses whatever hurt or emotion is causing her to have clouded judgment and to resort to this level of dialogue.

One evening, I got a text from Jess.

"I am going to kill myself" is all it said.

After calling her immediately and talking to her mom, Jess's reason was revealed. She had gotten grounded from the Internet for the rest of the day. She reached out to me to let me know she was going to kill herself because she got grounded.

Was she truly going to attempt suicide? I'm not sure. Obviously, I wouldn't take that risk. But is it possible that this might become so common for some parents or other adults that it could desensitize them to an actual threat? So I started asking myself whether it is possible for us to reverse this idea of attention-seeking technique.

Working with Jess was a long, hard process. After two suicide attempts, hospitalization, and multiple family sessions, we were able to break down some barriers that helped her parents see her with a new perspective. Jess's relationship with her parents has strengthened, and she no longer has suicidal ideation lingering in her day-to-day life. While she continues to struggle with hard times and bad moments, she now feels safe and important to her parents, so she can go to them when having dark thoughts. Finding acceptance within her own family system helped her organize her thoughts and emotions, making her hard life much more manageable.

Social Media

> *"I have a love/hate relationship with Snapchat. It's like I hate it but I can't stop checking it and wanting it. Every time I get on, I feel fine. But the minute I put my phone down, I feel horrible."*
>
> —17-YEAR-OLD FEMALE WHO SUFFERS FROM
> DEPRESSION AND ANXIETY

Added to our lives back in the early 2000s, social media has become the platform for socializing, news, marketing, and business. It has created the idea of a digital existence, and some users actually feel nonexistent without it. With a world full of loneliness and longing for attention, social media has become the quick and easy way to get just that.

Social media has created five big problems in our culture:

- No need to connect face to face
- Unrealistic comparisons
- Social life on 24/7
- "Mean" people have a safe place to say hurtful comments with little to no consequences
- Phone addiction

It was once about connection

Social media was created to connect people. When Facebook first came about, it was exclusively for college students, and the only picture on a person's page was their profile picture. It was a great way to keep in contact with friends from high school, and it helped connect freshmen who were struggling making new friends with other freshmen. It helped students in class contact other students about upcoming tests and projects. And no one had to worry about strangers from outside the community because you had to have a college email to be on there.

But, as with most things, it evolved. Social media became more than just Facebook. Facebook opened its doors to all individuals, not only college students. It changed from just profile pictures to pictures of everything. They added a newsfeed and pop-up ads. It went from a means of reaching out to people telling you what they ate for dinner. It changed from personal profiles to business profiles. All of these changes were ostensibly still intended to connect people. But do they?

Then you add in all the other social media platforms. Many people even have multiple accounts on each platform. And for the record, I am not anti–social media. I use Facebook, Instagram, and even Snapchat. What I am against is social media becoming the sole form for young individuals to connect. Connecting online is certainly a level of connection but not the kind of connection that gives you the satisfaction of feeling truly important to someone else in your life.

Comparisons

Although we know that what is seen on social media isn't always a true depiction or the whole experience of someone's everyday life or struggle, it seems to be easily forgotten in the middle of scrolling and self-loathing. Don't get me wrong; I don't think people should be putting all their dirty laundry on social media, and I find myself very annoyed by those who do, but for whatever reason, it is easy for individuals, especially young adolescents, to forget that the majority of others are posting *only* the good stuff. Individuals then find themselves believing that their "friend" is living this fantasy life while they are stuck in this hellhole of unrealistic comparisons. It can get quite depressing.

I've fallen into that myself. I had my first son when I was fairly young (24) and remember many late nights and early mornings scrolling through Facebook while feeding him and seeing all of my "friends" traveling to amazing places and enjoying amazing date nights and amazing experiences and having amazing jobs and amazing boyfriends or husbands sans kids, and there I was—overweight, fighting with my husband, sleep deprived, and feeling stuck in a routine that wasn't very amazing. Why were others living this amazing life and I wasn't? Why was I dwelling on that? It took a bit of personal growth for me to realize that my perception of my amazing friends was solely based on the Facebook evidence. How had I let myself become so delusional and naive? It is the world that we live in.

At 24, I was susceptible to this hellhole of unrealistic comparisons. Now, imagine being 13, dealing with all the natural big insecurities and confusions, trying to find yourself as an individual, and then piling social media on top of that. That's exactly what is happening. Handing over a smartphone to our young kids and allowing social media to be in their life is making the dreaded teenage years even worse. Today, while teenagers are discovering their individualism, they are intertwining their digital identity, and for many, that becomes their sole identity.

Too much drama

When I was in high school and dealing with stupid drama that was very real to me (I can call it stupid because I'm talking about my own experience here), I was able to go home on Friday and not have to deal with that drama if I didn't want to. I could choose to spend time with my family and distance myself from friends. That rarely happened because I was a social butterfly and wasn't super fond of my family at the time, but it did happen. Or if I was grounded, which I was a lot, I didn't have to sit at home sulking while knowing what all of my friends were doing. I could actually enjoy a movie with my parents, trying not to be mad at them and to not obsess over what I was missing. I didn't have any evidence of what I was missing out on. Even with instant messaging, I would sit at home and chat with others who were also sitting at home, not with anyone who was out and about.

But, today, drama can't be avoided. If a teen isn't invited to a party, whether through a malicious act or accident, they are reminded of that through Snapchat and Instagram. They can't escape it. It follows them home. Have you ever not been invited to something? I have, and it hurts. However, when I was in high school, I didn't find out about it until Monday at school. Today, kids are finding out about it as it's happening, and it ruins their weekend. It keeps them up at night feeling worthless and lonely. We felt all of those feelings, but we at least got breaks from it.

Cyberbullying

It has become common for people to be able to bully, harass, and abuse others from any location in the world. Social media is the perfect place for hurt people to hurt other people. There are so many hurt people in this world, and for many, social media has become their outlet. They don't have to directly confront someone; they can hide behind a screen and don't have to make eye contact. They get to act tough or say the clever comeback that they had time to think of instead of being clever on the spot. They become ruthless. They are nasty. Nothing gets held back.

If someone's digital identity, which has become their most important identity, becomes the target for someone who is hurting behind a screen, they will be publicly shamed, and it is as if their entire world comes crashing down. They have built a world for themselves that, once it has been depleted (by cyberbullying), they experience humiliation on a grander scale. That feeling of defeat and humiliation can be so dark and overwhelming that many go to the thought of suicide just to stop the pain.

Once someone begins the creation of their digital identity, they instantly become prey on the Internet. Remember when AOL first came out and everyone was fearful of chat rooms? I know my parents sat me and my siblings down to give us a good lesson on staying away from chat rooms because of the horrible people that could potentially be in them. Today, we are handing our kids a small device that fits in their hands with numerous platforms for those "horrible" predators to have direct access to their hearts and minds. And let's not forget: All of these issues with social media and drama and cyberbullying wouldn't be such a big issue if not for a much larger issue of phone addiction.

Phone addiction

As a parent, there is nothing like some peace and quiet after a long day. There are great benefits that have come with smart devices and our children using them. It creates such a calm and quiet environment. However, and I know you don't want to hear this, but there are some pretty dangerous consequences coexisting with that peace and quiet. More and more, I am seeing how addictive technology and smartphones are. Many of my clients (and—be honest—many of the rest of us) are openly addicted to their phones. I've had clients describe anxiety attacks from being away from their phones, whether that was because they couldn't communicate with their friends, help a friend through a hard time, or felt disconnected from their digital identity. There are studies on the effects of social media and technology on the brain.[6]

Dopamine is a chemical the brain releases when we feel pleasure. A substance such as cocaine causes the brain to release dopamine. When we pick up our phones and check social media for likes, our brains release dopamine just as it does with cocaine. Many individuals in today's culture are addicted to social media or the Internet. The good news is that this is a process addiction, which means we can still use smart devices and have the convenience of technology while working on recovery; no one has to quit cold turkey. The bad news is that it's a process addiction. You *can't* quit cold turkey, which makes it much harder to find balance to get rid of the addiction.

The chemical that releases when we connect with people is oxytocin. Some call it the "cuddle chemical." It's what couples feel after having sex. It's what kids feel after getting a hug from mom. It's the "I feel safe and good and happy all at once" chemical. We can even get it by just making eye contact with someone or holding hands or even sitting next to someone we care about. Through technology, social media particularly, we are attempting to connect. And we are succeeding to a certain degree. We are getting that dopamine fix but no oxytocin.[7] It is impossible to get that through social media and technology.

If we were to compare the behavior of someone addicted to cocaine with someone addicted to screens, they actually look very similar. They both need their drug all throughout the day, are happiest when they have

6   Nicholas Kardaras, "It's 'digital heroin': How screens turn kids into psychotic junkies," https://rccss.org/wp-content/uploads/2018/01/DigitalSafety/Digital-Heroin.pdf; and Adrian F. Ward, Kristen Duke, Ayelet Gneezy, and Maarten W. Bos, "Brain Drain: The Mere Presence of One's Own Smartphone Reduces Available Cognitive Capacity," *Journal of the Association for Consumer Research* 2, no. 2 (April 2017): 140-154. https://www.journals.uchicago.edu/doi/abs/10.1086/691462.

7   "Why Are Kids Addicted to Smartphones? Dopamine Surges," WebWatcher, https://www.webwatcher.com/blog/why-are-kids-addicted-to-smartphones-dopamine-surges; Katie Hurley, "Teenage Cell Phone Addiction: Are You Worried About Your Child?" Psycom, https://www.psycom.net/cell-phone-internet-addiction; and Trevor Haynes, "Dopamine, Smartphones & You: A battle for your time," blog, http://sitn.hms.harvard.edu/flash/2018/dopamine-smartphones-battle-time.

it, but they experience depression at the exact same time—isolation and more depression. And it's even worse when they don't get it. The tantrums and the fits are just ridiculous. Even my teenage clients can't handle the thought. They go into uncontrollable rages when they get it taken away. Multiple suicide attempts nationwide, and some completions, have been over phones. It sounds ridiculous, but if all the person's perceived happiness is absorbed from one source and that source gets taken away, they go through withdrawals.

I was recently talking with a colleague who has a 12-year-old daughter. She, like me, doesn't want her kids to have smartphones just yet, so she allows her daughter to have a flip phone for now. A flip phone can do all the things that are necessary at that age for emergencies, and it works for calls and texts.

The problem, however, is my colleague's daughter is the only one in her circle of friends who doesn't have an iPhone. She's embarrassed of her flip phone, and when she and her friends all hang out, they don't really talk with each other, because they are all doing things on their phone. So not only is she feeling left out and embarrassed, but now she's bored to pieces when hanging out with them.

My colleague and many other parents I speak to feel torn in this situation. If that is how teens are connecting, you don't want to isolate them. But smartphones are doing so much harm for their brains and their social skills. Which is the lesser of two evils? Is it possible to allow the smartphone and create strict limits? Or will that do the same thing as the flip phone? Is it possible that we can get enough parents on board and not allow our kids to have smartphones at such a young age?

We are all free to make our own parenting choices, but if something so easily accessible has the same effects as cocaine, I have to question whether parents know the repercussions and are able to make an informed decision. It's comparable to handing your car keys over to your 12-year-old, with no driving lessons, and just letting them take the wheel. That is exactly what is happening today, and it is only part of what has created the rise in suicidal ideation, suicide attempts, and completed suicides among teens and young adults today.

We were out to eat at a food truck, and my 8-year-old ran to me all sweaty and red in the face. He just needed to hydrate, and then he was going to go back out to play with the other kids. When he was in between gulps, he said, "Mom, look at all these kids on their technology. Why are they doing that? We're right over there having fun!" My heart was full when he said that to me. He was experiencing the joys that come from physical activity and connecting with others.

To help your own children avoid all the pitfalls of social media, keep them off of it until an appropriate age. Teach them first how to navigate real social interaction; then introduce them to social media and the Internet.

Pressure

"I don't understand. One minute she's nice, and the next, she's a bitch. Can you please help her see that she needs to be respectful and contribute to the house and keep her grades up and be involved in school and figure out what college she's going to go to and do better in volleyball and stop hanging out with her dramatic group of friends?"

—MOTHER OF A 12-YEAR-OLD SIXTH GRADER

visited my family doctor who loves to discuss social situations and issues every time I see him. One day, he asked about suicidal clients, and that discussion led to him handing me an article. The article was written from the viewpoint of trying to understand an ongoing suicide cluster in Silicon Valley. High school students were jumping in front of trains.

School has become outrageously intense. At least, here where I live in Texas it has. When my son started kindergarten, it was nothing like it was when I was in kindergarten, circa 1991. I remember kindergarten as half day, naps, play, ABCs, and Goldfish cracker snacks. Today, it is a full seven hours with only a 30-minute lunch and a 30-minute recess. The other six hours are dedicated to work, work, work. My sweet 6-year-old boy had such a hard time adjusting. He used words like "exhausted" and "frustrated" and "stressed." Already, at such a young age, he's lacking balance. And he's not even involved in any extracurriculars yet, nor does he really have homework yet. So what do middle school students feel—or junior high or high school? I can't imagine the amount of pressure and exhaustion they experience on a daily basis.

Our children are exhausted

Did you know that adolescents need 10–12 hours of sleep in a 24-hour period to truly feel rested, to keep their hormones somewhat stable, and to allow their brains to develop properly? Is that even possible? Not with all that we have to do in a day. I constantly hear about how tired my clients are. Some of that exhaustion is definitely self-induced: "Ugh, I stayed up till three in the morning watching YouTube and then realized I didn't finish my project, so I did that and finally fell asleep at 4:30 and woke up again at 6:00." Well, okay; that's a no-brainer. Others truly strive for a 10-hour sleep, but no matter how hard they try, they can't get everything they need to do that day finished in time to get to bed at a decent hour.

When my husband and I first married and had our first son, my husband was working more than 90-hour weeks. He was waking up at 5:00 a.m. to get to work by 6:30, to then continue working until around 11:00 p.m. (many nights, he would work much later), and then would come home, crash for a few hours, and get up again at 5:00. Anyone who knew he was doing this would constantly tell him things like, "Oh, man, that's not healthy. You've got to figure out a new schedule or a way to exist without so much work and exhaustion." They'd show sympathy. There was grace and mercy for him and the understanding that all other areas of his life were not possible. He was drowning in work and unhealthy.

We live in a go, go, go world

I can't help but recognize the similarities between my husband's schedule and lifestyle back then and today's teenagers' attempts to keep up. But teenagers aren't given the same grace and mercy my husband was. They don't feel understood or get sympathy for their busy lifestyle. They don't hear that it isn't healthy and that they need to find balance. They hear comments more along the lines of "Buck up, and deal with it" or "Welcome to the real-world, kid" or "There's no way you're tired; you don't know what real exhaustion feels like." On top of that, they aren't relieved of any area of their life by a spouse, partner, or family member. They have to keep up with school, stay involved, establish and maintain good and strong relationships with every human being in their life—and the list goes on and on and on.

Ethan is a junior in high school and on the lacrosse team. At 5:40, Ethan wakes up and attempts to eat breakfast and get ready for school. At 6:15, he needs to be out the door to pick up a friend that he carpools with. If they arrive at school by 7:10, they can socialize a little before the bell rings at 7:20. He goes through the day, trying to finish homework for one class during another so he doesn't have to squeeze it in later in the day. At 2:30, the last bell rings, and school is out, but lacrosse practice starts at 2:50. He's in practice until 5:00 and gets on the bus for an away game at 6:30. The game ends at 9:00, and the bus takes him back to school, where he carpools home. Once he's home—around 10:00—he heats up a dish, physically and mentally exhausted, and sits to quickly eat. While he's eating, he checks his Snapchat and Instagram pages. He has numerous direct messages (DMs) and texts that he wants to respond to. This process takes an hour, and he gets lost in the world of social media seeing what others are up to and texting with a girl he has been talking to, who, by the way, is pissed because he's just now responding, and she knows that he's had his phone on him most of the day, other than during the game. His mom is also upset with him because he's always on his phone—"No phone at the table!"—and because he got a B on his English quiz today. She also doesn't understand why he didn't bring the trash can in when he got home this evening and reminds him, with an annoyed, condescending tone, that he has things to do around the house; he can't just be on his phone all day. He takes a quick shower, but he still needs to study for the next day's chemistry and precalculus tests, and he has some history homework he wasn't able to finish at school. As he's studying for his exams, he falls back into the social media world after a friend sent him a funny meme, and he tries to smooth things over with that girl who's giving him grief. He finally falls asleep around 1:00, giving up on studying and giving up fighting his exhaustion. Then the day repeats: He wakes up again at 5:40 to half-heartedly finish his history homework and then be out the door again by 6:15.

I'm not saying it's lacrosse's fault, I'm not implying it's his mom's fault or that she shouldn't be upset with him, and I'm not blaming it completely on social media or phones. This is one of those seasons when life is hardest. I'm not even suggesting that much change from his routine exactly (other than trying to get more sleep and balance) but what I am suggesting is that, as parents, we need to recognize that our children are struggling. Life is as hard for them as it is for you—maybe harder. They live a life that is exhausting. It's different from the life you are living, but that doesn't mean that it isn't hard and that, somehow, they should just "buck up." Not only are they not getting enough rest and sleep, but they are also trying to live up to the immense pressure that has been placed on them, all on four or so hours of sleep. Parents are right there to tell them when they mess up or have the wrong thought process, but their stress levels are high. Their anxiety is high. Their motivation is low, due to exhaustion. Their ambition is fluid. Their moods are all over the place, and nobody can seem to figure out why. I frequently hear from my clients "I don't know why I have anxiety" or "I don't know why I'm so stressed and so exhausted."

Parents' part

I usually get to meet my clients at this point in their lives—full of anxiety and exhaustion. Their parents bring them in, saying things like, "I don't know why she has to be so rude to me. Like, the other day, she just snapped at me when I asked what she did at school. And she doesn't get anything done. She's so unproductive. No motivation. When I was her age, I had so much more going on, but for some reason, she can't handle it. I don't understand."

You take your job as a parent seriously—you are emotionally attached, and rightfully so—and are fearful your child will fail. As an outsider, I can see what is happening. Although we want our children to be perfect, the best version we can mold them into before they leave the nest, it's impossible. And sometimes, we need that reminder. We need to remember to incorporate a no, no, no lifestyle in this world of go, go, go for balance. If our world is filled with too much pressure (academic, social, internal, and family expectations), is it possible for parents to relieve some of that burden a little?

With some validation, understanding, and empathetic listening, we can begin to teach our children balance within their lifestyle and how to focus on strengths rather than the unreachable desire for perfection.

PART 2

What to Do

Now that you have an idea of the problems teens are facing today and what is happening in our culture and how it is negatively affecting them, it's time to talk about what we do about it. Some of the answers may seem like common sense, or you may already have some ideas floating around your head about what can be done. I encourage you to use this as a guidebook and reminder for how to address each issue, as well as the bigger problem as a whole. It's time for intentional parenting. This is not a one-answer solution. There are multiple contributing influencers; therefore, there are multiple aspects of our solution. All of the factors need to be considered when taking action. Although this is a parenting book, most of what I share is helpful for all people, no matter their age. Parents, you should practice what you preach by making your own life more balanced!

I treat the teenagers I work with like young adults. I like to break things down into simple goals. From there, we can build up smaller goals to get to the main one. Our main goal here is to build connections and resilience in order to help your teen become successfully independent.

Your teen is a human being who has opinions and thoughts that are very adult-like, because—guess what—they're turning into an adult! This is a good thing. If they are willing to open up to you, which is a very mature and adult-like act, then you have to respect that decision, honor the maturity, and prepare yourself to learn some new aspects about your teenager's life. Some may be shocking, and some may create pride in you, as a parent. Regardless, allow this opportunity to get to know and understand your daughter or son *now*.

Many call the teenage years "toddler phase 2," and it's true. Your little innocent sweet baby is now changing rapidly into an adult who isn't as innocent. They've heard all the words; they've seen all the things and done many of them already. Their innocence is gone. That doesn't mean they are a bad teen; it means you need to stop being oblivious or naive about life's realities. Get to know your teenager as they are changing. Open your mind to the human being they are today, not the idyllic child you picture them as. And just know: They might be a different version of themselves next month.

If we are going to be talking about awareness and what the symptoms of suicide look like, we *must* balance that with preventative care—and not just, "Okay, if you see these symptoms, get them to a therapist." That's not going to do much. And with the way things are going, the symptoms are harder to see.

We need to learn how to talk to our kids about suicide and how to determine the right time for the conversation. We need to learn how to engage with our kids to be part of this cultural shift by allowing them to share their thoughts and opinions. We need to spread the information of this cultural shift to parents of young kids so they can start working on these things *now*. We need to explore healthy coping skills with our kids at a young age (it's never too late, though) so they don't have to try and figure it out alone or feel alone or end up in a hospital and only connect with others who are in the hospital as well.

Frosted glass

Think back to when you had your first baby—the first week, month, maybe even the first year was hard, to say the least. You were getting little sleep, you had new responsibilities to take care of that you've never had to worry about before—I mean, a human being. You put yourself on the back burner. Most likely, you tried to keep up with everything else in your life—the condition of your house, your relationships with friends, your relationship with your spouse—all before brushing your teeth. Everything started to show the effects. Your priorities changed. You were just so tired and filled with overwhelming anxiety.

Then there was that one "friend" or your mother or the aunt who maybe talks a little too much—that person who compares her life to everything you're going through. You know who I'm talking about. I bet you're thinking of that person now, aren't you? We've all got them in our lives. They love us, but they can be insensitive.

You confided in her that you were so tired and stressed, and maybe you even started to cry while talking to her because you noticed you didn't have any clean bottles and the baby needed to eat and the sink was filled with dirty dishes.

Her response? "You're tired?! Girl, you don't even know what tired is!"

What did you feel when she dismissed everything you were going through? It would be natural to feel annoyed, angry, inadequate, shamed, disappointed, and not heard or understood. Maybe she thought she was being supportive; however, in that emotional state, you started to get offended and distanced yourself. No matter her intentions, there's a good chance you conditioned yourself to not take what she says too seriously, and each time she talks, you want to roll your eyes.

It would've been so much nicer if your aunt offered help around the house, let you, as a new mother, know that it's okay to cry and feel unbalanced because she is confident that you're going to be fine, just as she was. She takes the pressure off. She offers you a compassionate and empathetic ear. She cleans those bottles as fast as she can, so she can hold that sweet baby while you go take a shower and nap or brush your teeth. If only your aunt had been there like that for you, you'd have no anger, no heightened anxiety, no feelings of failure or disappointment. Instead, you'd feel comforted and understood.

This is how your teen feels every time you dismiss their exhaustion and stress. Just like you with that new baby, your teenager isn't sleeping well. If she isn't fueled with good, healthy food, she could start to feel more sluggish and uncomfortable. Do we need to discuss self-image and weight issues too? She cries a lot—over things that seem so ridiculous to you. I remember crying as a teen when my towel fell off the towel rack, and I had to pick it up and put it back. I was overwhelmed by the feeling that nothing right was happening in my life; even the towel betrayed me. The other day, my 2-year-old cried because he dropped a sock right in front of him and threw himself on the floor screaming and crying and wanted me to pick it up and hand it to him. I mean . . . What!? Get it together, kid! That's what we think sometimes, right?

Is it possible, that in her world, it *is* that stressful? She has nothing to compare it to. Just like when you had that new baby and were looking at her beautiful little eyelashes while she was sleeping so soundly, thinking "Oh, God, please get me through this. I am so tired, and I want to keep her safe forever. How am I ever going to get sleep? How am I going to fix my resentment toward my husband?" (Don't lie. It was there.)

Your child is experiencing something new—and often: new emotions, new responsibilities, new stressors. Being a freshman in high school is a totally new ball game. She'll have new fears, new unknowns, new friends, and grief over lost friends. It's a lot. The last thing you want your child to feel is annoyed, angry, inadequate, shamed, disappointed, and not heard or understood.

What if I told you that there is a wall between the two of you that only you can tear down? This wall is somewhat see-through, like frosted glass, and separates you from your former self, which in turn, separates you from your teen because it keeps you disconnected from what it is like to be a teenager. You can see yourself on the other side, but it's all a bit fuzzy. You can see a shape, you can distinguish colors, but you can't see the details.

You can remember your teenage years, but because of your growth and experience, you are unable to see the details of associated events—the very real, intense emotions you felt, the dynamic of relationships you were in, the stress you felt at the time and reactions you had in those distant moments. You can now look back at some of these memories and think of how you would do them differently. You now have knowledge that has made certain situations easier to deal with today. You can probably remember something as hard or sad, but you can't literally attach and feel today the emotions you felt at the time. Although you might abstractly recognize the figure on the other side of the glass, it just isn't completely clear.

Each year that you grow further from your teenage years, the glass becomes more frosted. This is a good thing. It symbolizes growth, strength, and healing. However, this comes with a negative (as most things do, right?). With that distance, you are unable to truly connect with what your teenager is going through today.

Not only do you have years of experience, but add in that today's culture is extremely different from when you were a young teen, and you are not the same person as your child either. Some of us still forget that: Your child is an individual person, not part of you. There will be things that you just can't understand, and they may react to situations differently from how you did. Maybe you can remember or relate in the abstract, but you don't actually know what they're going through.

Instead of lecturing, trying to relate (through one-ups or put-downs), or dismissing your teen's problems, try offering an empathetic ear. Listen. Validate their feelings, and concentrate on those feelings rather than the content.

The best thing with the frosted glass is that you *can* see the image. You can remember your own story and heartache, so it gives you the ability to understand, empathize, and connect with your child when they are feeling something big. You just have to remember that it isn't about your heartache; it's about theirs. By expressing empathy and listening intently, you'll have a higher chance of forging a connection with your kids. Sometimes that can turn into a conversation where you do share your hardships and your memories, and they get to see a version of you that they weren't allowing themselves to see before.

Any response you choose must be genuine and from a comfortable place for you, but you might start with something like these:

> "Ah, I am so sorry you are going through this. It must feel overwhelming. Is there anything I can do to help?"

> "I want to hear more about what's going on with you and your friends. It sounds like it must be a lot. We all go through social struggles, so I know it can be hard, but I don't know what it's like for you. I want to hear more about how you're handling it."

> "You seem like you're going through something. I hate seeing you this way and wish I could help. I'd really love to hear what's going on with you, but if you're not ready, that's fine. I'd like for you to figure out a way to not talk to me like that when I ask you to help around the house. If I have done something that is making you mad, can we talk about it? If it has nothing to do with me, I'd like you to know that it hurts me when you snap at me that way."

Notice that there was nothing that said "I'm the expert of your life" or "Let me tell you about what happened to me so I can prove that I know what you're going through." Rather, the focus is on the emotion the child is feeling and your interest in how they are handling it or feeling at the moment.

Parenting philosophy

Determining your parenting philosophies is important because it will become the foundation of the goals you have for your child. This will help with almost all situations that arise during your parenting journey. Because each child is different and because we have to address each situation as unique, this is a good starting point to help guide how to handle whatever gets thrown your way.

We can't produce perfect humans, so we need to narrow down what you expect from your child. I always ask parents to come up with three main parenting philosophies that they believe in and want for their child. What are the basic, main goals that you have for raising your child? Imagine the moment when you are leaving them at their dorm freshman year. You can turn and look at them and think, *Through all the hard times and life lessons thus far, I have done my part to raise a(n) _____ individual.*

Do you want your child to have a kind heart? Do you want your child to just stay alive? Are your goals for them to be smart and excel academically or become insanely rich?

Here are some examples to get you thinking:

- Kindhearted
- Compassionate
- Giving
- Helpful
- Safe
- Healthy
- Wealthy
- Empathetic
- Understanding
- Independent
- Strong
- Religious
- Ambitious
- Driven
- Motivated
- Encouraging
- Scrupulous

Choose two or three options or add some of your own. Now, imagine placing each word you've chosen into the sentences below.

My parenting philosophy

"I will do my part to raise a(n) _____ individual."

"I will approach life lessons with my child to build a(n) _____ individual."

"As a parent, most importantly, I want my child to be _____."

Now you have your foundation. When fights break out between your kids who won't share, when your son comes home with a failing grade, when your child is feeling bored, when your daughter is in a fight with her best friend, when your teen comes home drunk, when your preteen is glued to her phone, you can begin with these three sentences. This is your guide to handling each situation that comes up throughout their years with you.

Recognize Your Influence

"It's like every time I try to do better, it's never enough. I can never meet their expectations. It's impossible and makes me really uncomfortable to be around them."

—14-YEAR-OLD STRUGGLING WITH SELF-HARM

I n order to make a change to help build connection and resilience, you have to look at your part as the parent. You're a smart person. I know that, and you know that. Your teen is a smart person as well. All I ask of you is to be patient with your teen, knowing that they are learning and growing every day emotionally, mentally, and physically. Find the patience to know that they are smart enough to learn from their mistakes. I know that's easier said than done, right?

It doesn't mean you can't be upset or affected. But you should keep your ultimate goal for your child in mind: that they become autonomous, independent, strong individuals. We can't lock them up in the tower for the rest of their lives. We have to find the comfort as their parent to let them grow and discover their purposes in life.

I am asking a lot from you in this book. I ask for your understanding and for your willingness to open up your mind so your teen can feel human during these years. But mostly, I ask for your sensitivity to your child and the emotions they are experiencing within. Set your own fear aside.

Fear-based parenting

When I was a kid, I couldn't wait to be a grown up. I dreamed it would be this amazing feeling of freedom, where I could say what I wanted and do what I wanted, and no one was going to stop me. I was eager to break down the doors to adulthood and finally get to live the happy life that I was meant to live. My parents were holding me back!

Are you laughing yet? Maybe you remember feeling some of the same, but now, as adults, we know that although we can say what we want and technically do what we want, those choices have consequences. But we don't tend to feel that same overwhelming sense of being controlled that we did as teenagers, and there's good reason for that.

Almost every moment and aspect of a child's world is controlled by someone else. From what they're allowed to say out loud to what they are eating for dinner to when they get to use the restroom, they have to ask permission or are simply told what they will do for everything. Adolescents are in transition: They want to make their own decisions, and they are finally getting a taste of independent decision-making, but many choices are still out of their hands. This makes them angry and annoyed. It pushes them to want to rebel or become defiant. What I find with my teen clients is that if they are open to learning how to control their emotional well-being and also to understand a few factors about their parents, their hard life tends to lean more on the good side than on the bad. I help them find a smoother path. Likewise, when their parents allow some of the control to gradually be placed in their child's hands, the relationship becomes stronger.

But in order to allow your teen to make their own choices, you have to admit first that you're scared. Being a mom or dad is really scary. From the moment you found out you were pregnant to this very moment realizing the culture that we live in. We cannot always protect our child from harm. We can do our best, but unfortunately, some things are out of our control, and that's terrifying. I call most parents' parenting style *fear-based parenting*. It isn't the best approach, but it's natural and common. No matter what kind of parent you are, how understanding you've become, there is fear weighing on your heart and mind. Your child or teen does not and will not understand this until they experience it themselves, which is exactly how it needs to stay. We don't need *everyone* on earth being scared! We have to balance out teenage fearlessness with some of our own fear.

With that said, some parents base most or all of their parenting decisions, interactions, choices, and communication techniques on that fear. Just as I mentioned before, hurt people hurt people. Fear is a form of hurt. When a kid runs across the street without looking, and the mom yells, "STOP IT! WHAT ARE YOU DOING?! OH, MY GOODNESS! YOU COULD'VE GOTTEN KILLED!! WHAT IS WRONG WITH YOU!? NEVER DO THAT AGAIN!" she has allowed fear to overshadow her parenting. Although she had every right to be scared in that moment, she's reacting within that fear. You feel that same fear when your kid is sneaking back in the house or not answering their phone and turned off their GPS or lying about who they hung out with and what they were doing. In your mind, your child could die.

I always explain to my young clients that although *they* knew where they were, and *they* knew they weren't doing anything too horrible, their parents' thoughts were literally along the lines of, "and he's probably dead in a ditch now" or "so she'll end up getting addicted to crack, pregnant, and homeless." It sounds dramatic, yes. They just had to drive their friend home and were 30 minutes past curfew and coincidentally their phone died, but this is where parents' thoughts go. Some of us have gotten good at controlling our anxiety and worry, but needless to say, it is natural for us to think of our child's safety. It is our biggest job as parents.

Sometimes, as parents, we need to let our kids know how scary something is by reacting to our own fear, hoping it scares the child as well (like running across the street without looking), but for most situations, the fear will get in the way of communicating with your child. Fear-based parenting can come across as if the parent doesn't actually care. Typically, as parents, when we react out of fear, we come across as angry or even sometimes with the condescending attitude of, "You're so dumb!" While we want the takeaway message to be clear, many times it's misinterpreted as "My dad thinks I'm dumb," or "My mom is mad at me."

Feel the fear, sure, but don't react within it. Regulate your own emotions, establish the intended lesson you want your child to grasp, and let your child know what needs to change in a controlled and reasonable tone. This is a good time to put focus back on your two or three core parenting philosophy goals we discussed earlier. With every situation that has ignited fear, you can hone in on what your big goals with your child are and keep the focus clear.

Communicating in this calm, reasonable manner with your child in a time of fear is a challenge; that's a definite. But if you can practice this style of parenting with calm and comforting intention as opposed to staying fear-based, the likelihood of your lesson being absorbed and heard is much higher.

What's more is that fear-based parenting doesn't apply just to our children's physical safety. It is present in almost every life lesson we teach them. It starts when they are babies with thoughts like *Oh, gosh, she doesn't listen to me when I tell her to put her shoes on. She's going to fail in school because she's a horrible listener* or *He just keeps hitting his brother and won't share. He's going to be a horrible person if I don't somehow figure out how to fix this now.* And as they become young adults, it continues: *He lied to me about what time band practice ended. What else is he lying to me about? My son is a liar. He must not respect me. He'll never understand what a big deal it is to have integrity in this world. He needs to respect his elders. He's doomed!* or *If they can't get through studying in high school, how are they ever going to make it through college?* or *He always loses his stuff and can't seem to figure out how to be organized. He's never going to make it in this world and is going to end up smoking weed and becoming a bum* or, one of the ultimate parenting fears, *I've failed as a parent.*

Once you've become aware of your intentions and fears, you can address the situation with a calm demeanor. This can make you seem detached or cold, and it obscures your fear—but that's the point. By not allowing your fear to permeate your communication with your teen, you make it easier for them to hear you. They can pay attention to *what* you say instead of how you say it.

The vision

The moment a woman finds out that she is pregnant, she begins having a vision of that child. She imagines how she'll parent, who they'll be, and what she wants for them. Sitting with parents, both the mom and the dad, I see time and time again how men don't experience this vision right away the way women do. Men don't always bond with the child until the baby is born. But for the women, the vision begins almost instantly. Even when they don't know the sex of the baby yet, their thoughts swirl around their mind, such as

- What am I going to do different from my parents?
- What am I going to do the same as my parents?
- What was good about my upbringing?
- What was bad about my upbringing?
- What can I provide for my family?
- What do I want for my sweet child?
- I will do anything for this new love of my life.

- He will go to Harvard.

- She will be beautiful and well liked by others.

- He will play football.

- She will be involved in dance, as I was.

- He will play an instrument.

- She will show interest in science.

- He will be a math whiz.

I hear parents say things like, "I just want him to be happy. If he doesn't like football, fine. But be productive." In theory, that's a great sentiment. But do they truly believe that that is all that they want for their child? I'm not so sure. There's a little bit of that vision the parents are still holding on to, unmet expectations for their child. They secretly wish their daughter played in the orchestra or their son was more involved in church youth group. What would it be like if we didn't hold on to our visions? Or better yet, what if we created a vision that focuses on our child's character instead of our fantasies for them?

When parents are able to recognize that the vision they may be holding on to isn't completely realistic, walls are knocked down almost immediately. Openness and acceptance become the focus, making connection and trust achieved easier within the relationship of parent and child.

Simply by becoming aware, parents can choose to react differently from here on out. Maybe you don't realize you're holding on to a vision or that you even had one to begin with. Becoming aware is the first step. You can then follow it by actively accepting your child for who they are today.

Don't be a hypocrite

"She's just so ungrateful," a parent of one of my clients said. "I take her to school every day, and she barely talks in the car. Then she slams the door without a simple 'Bye, Mom!' or 'Thank you!' Why is it that she can't even say thank you?"

No, you don't *have* to take your child to school every day. However, you do, and it has become an expectation. It has become part of your parenting duties, and if you've always done it, your child doesn't know any other way. Whether it's an expectation, privileged or not, or an occasional favor, your child should absolutely recognize it and express their thanks. The problem is, they don't get thanks from you either. You take just as much for granted in your relationship as they do.

Hypocrite is a word I frequently hear come out of teenagers' mouths. I remember feeling it toward my parents as well. Seeming to be a hypocrite will frustrate your teen to no end and may destroy your credibility with them. And they're right!

Sometimes I catch myself feeling irritable about something or annoyed that my son has asked me the same question a billion times. I might snap—sometimes I even yell—but in my mind, I've already answered the question, so he should expect me to react that way. If my son spoke to me the way I've spoken to him in those moments, he would get in trouble. It wouldn't matter how bothered he was or what was going on in his world; he needs to learn to mind his manners and speak to me with respect.

When I catch myself reacting to my kids in a way I would never tolerate from them, I try to call myself out on it. *You're being a hypocrite*, I tell myself. *Stop it.* If there are moments when I can't self-regulate, how could I expect my 6-year-old to do it better than me? And when they don't meet my expectations, I follow that with shame and discipline? Of course, we want to and need to teach our children how to self-regulate, but we also need to do our part of self-regulating. Hypocrisy only leads to resentment. And the last thing I want is for my children to resent me.

My hope is that, with some awareness, different perspectives, and an open mind, you will recognize whether or not you fall into this category. If your child described you in this manner, would it be possible to take an honest look at yourself and make the change needed for a healthier relationship? Modeling behavior is important in the parent–child relationship. If you are asking your child to make behavioral growth but aren't displaying that yourself, can you expect much change on their end? (The answer is no.)

Respect

Respect needs to be mutual. I know that doesn't always sit well as the parent, especially a fear-based parent, but hear me out. Your relationship with your child does not have to be a power struggle. You do not need to show them who's boss. That philosophy only pisses them off, and it would piss you off too if you were treated that way by your boss, your spouse, your sibling—anyone!

Your child does need to listen to you, display gratitude, and appreciate you, but they will not absorb a darn thing or become grateful if you go in thinking you need to dominate—I promise you. You're allowed to get upset with your child—don't get me wrong—just like they should be allowed to get upset with you. But just as you practice showing respect at work, in church, or toward your spouse, it needs to be practiced toward your children as well. Respect your child as a human. Respect your child as someone who may not agree with what you have to say all the time. In turn, they will begin imitating that same behavior when they are upset and reciprocate the respect.

I realize this is a hard concept to live by. It's easier as parents to sometimes reply with, "Because I said so!" or "Don't ask why; just do as I say." Sometimes, there are certain rules that we know our children won't understand, so they just need to abide by them. That way of thinking will only go on for so long before you begin to experience the rebuttal. This is actually a strong quality your child *should* develop. They are experiencing being treated a way that they don't like, and they want you to know, whether it be an eye roll, a dramatic scream, or a slam of the door. Is it disrespectful? Yes. This is a good opportunity to recognize their lack of respect for you and address it *with* respect:

"I know you don't like that I just told you to clean your room before you could play video games, but I don't care for the way you just responded to me. You're allowed to not like what I am telling you, but it's not okay to talk to me that way. I'd like for us to talk freely about how we feel but not if it's going to hurt the other's feelings. I know I do this sometimes to you as well. Can we both cool down and talk more about this in a few minutes?"

Foster Connection

"I feel like such a loser because I have, like, only one friend. All my friends are so fake and superficial. And anytime I try to talk to my mom, she just lectures me. I can't tell her anything."

—17-YEAR-OLD STRUGGLING WITH DEPRESSION AND SELF-HARM

Whether your child is little or in their teens, building a personal connection needs to start today. No matter how busy you all are, no matter how annoyed they may seem to be with you, connection starts by parents engaging with their kids. Personal connection is the antidote to your teen feeling a lack of attention and for the desperate quest for connection on social media as well. If they are growing up in this world where attention is almost impossible, it is our job to give our kids that attention so they know they are important and valued. Build their self-confidence by showing them they are important to you; the best way to do that is to genuinely connect with them. It all starts at home, within the family system.

What is our goal when spending time and talking with our kids? For me, it's to provide a comforting and safe relationship so they feel confident to have open, authentic conversations. Most individuals connect best when *doing* something. Staring at each other and forcing a conversation doesn't do it. Friends don't meet up to just stare at each other. Friends meet up to get a cup of coffee or take a spin class or go shopping. I'm pretty sure married couples don't hire a babysitter to just look at each other in awkward silence; date night is for getting out and doing something together. Kids connect with other kids through play or books or music or video games. Your child may not be very vocal or may even come across as if they are uninterested, but the truth is that they want to talk to you; you need to find a way to connect with their interests. Building a strong connection starts with simply spending time with your child in their comfort zone.

If your son enjoys playing video games, you can sit and join, watch and learn, or ask him about it when he isn't playing. If your 4-year-old likes to color, if your daughter likes to be outdoors, if all of your kids enjoy board games, if they like to spend time in their room, whatever it is, ask for permission to join and just be with them. Do it as often as you can.

I remember when I was studying in graduate school, learning how much time parents should spend with their child on a daily basis. It seemed daunting and overwhelming, and at that time, I only had two kids. I find that sort of quota-based goal unrealistic, especially if you have more than one child, you work, and you live in today's high-speed lifestyle. Carving out time for your kids is wonderful. If you can do that, do it. If that is hard to balance, try to figure out how you make it part of your routine. I like to spend about 10 minutes with each of my boys at bedtime reading, singing songs, and asking about their day. I work two evenings a week, so I get to do this with them five nights out of the week. There are nights that I'm unavailable, wiped out, on a date with my husband, or caught up at work and can't do it. That's okay with me, because I know it's just an exception out of our usual routine.

And you better believe that on days that they are acting up and aren't listening well, nights that I just want to get downstairs to pour myself a glass of . . . water . . . I power through the struggle and resist the urge to yell and turn all the lights out to give them a little extra attention. Those crazy days and nights of bad behavior are when they need that extra hug, extra book, and extra assurance that you love them.

Just the other night, I went in to read to my 6-year-old. He asked to play with a few LEGOs before we turned the light out, and so I found myself locked in trying to complete a LEGO project with him. In the middle of looking for a piece that we needed, he asked me all about girls, when he's allowed to kiss one, and what it's like to get married. I went in there to read him a book and play a little LEGOs, and it ended up in an age-appropriate sex talk! When you remind yourself that your child is just another human with their own opinions and perceptions in this world, you can genuinely take interest in who they are and who they are growing into.

How to effectively communicate

We can't necessarily make kids stop talking about things and stop spreading the idea of suicide. But we can help understand what's going on with them hormonally and developmentally. With an open mind, I encourage parents, teachers, principals, coaches, counselors, and pastors to invest some time into understanding what teens are absorbing in their day-to-day lives and this begins with effective communication.

Here is a start for getting your mind and heart in the right place when going into conflict or a time for active listening. This is good for all relationships, not just a parent–child relationship. It's called LOVE communication:

LOVE communication

- Listen actively with a clear mind and an

- Open heart for acceptance.

- Validate the emotion behind the behavior, and then

- Express with your response and thoughts in a calm manner.

The emotion behind the behavior is what needs recognition. Bad behavior is not good, no, but if you give the emotion behind it more attention than the behavior, you will see a shift in behavior from negative to positive. You give attention to the emotion by validating it. If you can learn how to recognize the emotion that is trying to be conveyed or the emotion that is behind the screaming, yelling, tantrums, and attitudes, you will break down walls—and fast. Validating someone's feeling lets the other person know that you hear what they are saying. You may not agree, but you understand that they are feeling an emotion and you need to understand that. Don't we all want—and deserve—to feel heard? Respecting each other means empathizing and allowing someone to be heard. Respect needs to be shared mutually in all relationships; whether you are 50 or 5, you deserve respect. And you deserve to be heard. Here are some example validations:

Your youngest screams, "He just took my car from me! Give it back!"

"Oh, no!" you say empathetically and then validate the feeling: "You're frustrated with him."

"Yeah! It's unfair. We're supposed to share!" See? Your child has opened up by explaining more about what has upset him.

So you continue to validate his feelings and confirm that you understand what he wants you to understand: "You feel that you should have the car longer and choose when to share it with him."

"Yeah!"

Typically, people's intentions are good. But the takeaway is what matters; it can make or break the conversation. Figuring out the intention, the root of the message your child is trying to convey, is where validation comes in handy. Validating is helpful to be sure your child's intended message is being received correctly.

If you start with something like "You need to get your homework done! We have a big weekend and you have that test on Monday! You're not going to have time to get it done on Sunday," typically, your teen will fire back a defensive reaction. They are defending not only that they don't want to work on their homework but also your perceived attack on their character. Many times, when we get into conflict with loved ones, our intended message is not heard. Instead, we perceive an attack, and a good intention can quickly get lost in a bad argument.

If you instead respond with, "You're feeling annoyed that I keep telling you to do your homework," that allows your child to agree or disagree. If they disagree, you can then see that what they said was not how you understood it. It works on the other end also. Maybe your intended message is not what they are understanding. Recognizing that we sometimes intend a specific message but it isn't always perceived correctly can help you as a parent when you feel your child is not hearing what you're saying. Many times, it can help you both avoid saying something hurtful.

Responding versus reacting

Learning the difference between responding and reacting is good for all relationship types. We tend to emotionally react much quicker than we respond. Maybe we didn't even hear a word they said, because we've been fueling our very clever reaction the whole time, or there's a slight chance we didn't let them finish, that we interrupted with our reaction and beat them to it so we wouldn't forget our very strong point. In this type of exchange, neither person will feel heard or understood, and the argument will drag out with an unsatisfactory—or no—resolution.

Reacting is quick and easy because you don't have to put much thought into it. You simply allow your emotions to take over, and before you know it, you're caught going in circles with whoever you're arguing with. Reacting is typically louder in volume and has a negative tone. It usually includes some accusations and assumptions. Reacting is allowing your emotions to take the wheel and drive the ship into the ground. It always shuts down the other person or ignites anger and defensiveness. It will quickly make a discussion turn into a fight. Your reaction includes your body language too: rolling the eyes, turning away, crossing the arms, loud sighs, and so on can set your teen off.

Responding, on the other hand, is different. Responding is the act of focusing on the end goal, your intended message, and signaling to the other person that you care about their point of view. Responding is a two-step process. It includes validating what you heard and *then* sharing your thoughts and opinions in a calm manner. The best part about it being a two-step process is that it slows down the conversation, so you have more time to think of how to compose your thoughts. If you focus on validating first, then you can make sure your emotions are in check and come up with an appropriate response. If we just react, it doesn't allow us to hear what the other person said; rather, it allows our emotions to take over the conversation. And we all know that sometimes our emotions, like anger, that come out in the conversation can be hurtful or irrelevant.

Whether we're aware of it or not, we all successfully respond instead of react when we communicate via email or text. This goes on the pro side of technological advances. Typically, if you were to receive an email from your upset boss, say, or angry partner, you literally can't react immediately. The email is not in real time. You read it first and then respond. Of course, you may be boiling up inside while reading it, but you are unable to interrupt and fire back in real time. You have to hear (read) everything they want you to hear before you share your thoughts. Most likely, you get your fingers ready to release that anger back. And sometimes you type away and hit send before thinking (I do not advise this). If you value that person or your job, you either wait to respond or you write, read, delete, edit, reread, delete, and so on. It prevents the emotional reaction from being expressed before you've carved it into a response.

Let's set up an example. With a scared, hesitant tone, your 16-year-old son shares with you that he's thinking of quitting the soccer team. He has played the sport since he was 3. You've spent countless hours dedicated to his soccer talent. You've spent thousands of dollars on uniforms, clubs, traveling, shin guards and orange slices. Your mind begins to flood with thoughts of fear. You don't want him to quit. You don't want your son to throw away all that hard work from the past 13 years. You don't want your son to be a quitter. What if your son is someone who just gives up when things don't go his way? Is this because he has a new girlfriend and wants to spend most of his time with her? Is it because he didn't get to start last game? These thoughts circle within you, and you want to share all of them with him. You're upset, sad, confused—too many emotions all at once.

One likely reaction might be "WHAT!? WHAT ARE YOU TALKING ABOUT? YOU LOVE SOCCER! YOU'RE NOT QUITTING. WE'VE PUT TOO MUCH TIME AND MONEY INTO THIS! YOU BETTER FIGURE IT OUT, BECAUSE YOU'RE NOT QUITTING ANYTHING!"

Example of an appropriate response, with validation would be more along these lines: "Oh, gosh. I am so confused, but thank you for telling me about this. You're feeling overwhelmed and really not liking soccer or your team right now. I want to hear more about what's going on. Now isn't the best time, but let's plan to talk after dinner. Maybe we can figure this out so you feel comfortable with your decision."

Notice how Mom is focusing on the emotion—not the behavior or an accusation. This is really hard to do, because, in our brain, we typically *are* reacting. But reacting doesn't help move the conversation along. It puts it at a halt or turns it into a fight, which is neither productive nor beneficial for anyone involved. The mom is open to the fact that her 16-year-old is his own individual and is experiencing one of those tough life experiences that he can potentially gain from. If the mom were to react, there is a stronger chance that he would struggle through that experience feeling alone rather than supported.

Maybe some of this scenario is unrealistic. As parents, you are human and allowed to feel angry and mad at your son. I'm not asking for you to become a robot with no emotions or a laid-back parent that allows their kid to do whatever they want. And vice versa for the teen. Teenagers and kids are allowed to feel angry or scared or sad too. But it's how we communicate those emotions that is important.

If you are so mad when you find something out that you can't respond at the moment, a simple postponement will help: "This is really shocking for me to hear right now, and I need to process this before we talk about it. I'm not really happy about this so please get your homework done, and I will begin dinner. Let's talk after dinner." The follow-up discussion can include validation and an appropriate response.

Build connection by giving attention

Recognizing your child's accomplishments, hard work, and positive attributes—not only academics—is a great way to build connection. How well your daughter supports her friends or how well your son plays with his little brother or how much you appreciate that all your kids clean their spot after dinner are all worthy of praise. Many times, we think, "I shouldn't thank them for that; they should be doing it anyway!" If we do things well and are not recognized, we can start to feel worthless and unnoticed. And teenagers and children are more sensitive than we adults tend to be.

For many teenagers, a lot of negative thoughts are swirling around within their minds throughout the day. They know they should've studied harder for that test. They now feel stupid and disappointed with themselves. They wish they looked different. They wish they talked differently. These concerns may seem like ridiculous insecurities to us, but our teens are dealing with them all day long. If they are not getting any positive statements from others, they will eventually feel flooded and hopeless.

But what if, every time they remember something (that they should remember anyway), it gets recognized and praised? Or what if they got a C on an English paper, but as their parent, you choose to admire all the hard work put into the paper or even a better grade that they received in a different class?

One of my favorite go-to books is *The 5 Love Languages* by Gary Chapman. It's great for couples, but did you know that he wrote one specifically for kids, as well as teens? It's a very simple read and extremely helpful. Understanding your child or teen's love language can make a noticeable difference. It starts with a simple question: "How do you know I love you?" Depending on their answer, you can figure out their love language. Once you are aware of how they feel love and how they show love, you can begin incorporating it into your daily routine with that child.

I strongly believe that relationships within the family system hold priority over outside relationships. And although we put a lot of emphasis on the husband and wife, we seem to not recognize that the parent–child relationship needs *just as much* attention. If you look at your relationship with your child or teen as needing as much (and oftentimes similar) effort and work as that with your spouse, it could potentially create a house where everyone feels important. If the foundation of relationships between family members is strong, conflicts can be handled effectively. If the foundation of the relationships between family members is weak, conflicts are going to be overwhelming, never-ending, and extremely draining on everyone.

Talking about the tough stuff

"I just want to die." Well, now, that's a scary statement to hear. Many adults who hear this are blinded by fear or struggle to figure out the best thing to say. Sometimes, we minimize the emotion expressed or dismiss it completely. No parent wants to hear something like this come out of their child's mouth, but dismissing it may later be your biggest regret.

One way or another, we have all felt desperation, hopelessness, and exhaustion. We are allowed to feel this way. Your teen is allowed to feel this way. It's what we do with that exhausted thought that makes a difference.

I always allow my clients true freedom of speech in my office, and I hear statements of release on a daily basis:

- "I just want to sleep through the next five months until summer."
- "I just want to run away and never come back."
- "Can someone put me in a coma, please?"
- "I just want to die."
- "I'd rather be dead."
- "Life sucks."
- "Just kill me now."
- "Ugh! I can't do life anymore."

My way of allowing this is by paying attention to and controlling my reaction so that I am not outwardly shocked by the statement. Many times, we hear these statements and our fear takes over our thoughts, jumping to conclusions such as, "Oh my gosh, you're depressed!" or "You're suicidal and need hospitalization immediately!"

Since exaggerated statements are natural ways of thinking when we are met with an exceptionally hard life stressor, I believe that, sometimes, we all just need a place to say it out loud. It is okay to say it and not actually *mean* that you literally want to die. During these hard times, it would be much easier to just sleep it off and wake up feeling better. Unfortunately, that isn't always possible. The good news is that sometimes it is! If you've had a rough day, sometimes we just need to call it a day and go to sleep so we can start with a refreshed mind tomorrow.

Regardless of what's got your child down, allow them to feel it, or at least recognize that it's there and that there isn't anything wrong with them for feeling that way. It's part of the process to feel better. We need to grant our children permission to feel and express such emotions. When we cut that off or don't allow the expression, anger and resentment will take over, creating a further distance in the relationship.

Allowing them to express their emotions is just the first step. It should not be ignored or dismissed. But what about when your child won't stop saying these things and is calling out for help? What do you do when your child comes to tell you that they are in a dark place and having these heavy thoughts? What if one of your kid's friends calls or texts to tell you this about your child?

First and foremost, control your reaction. Don't let your fear take over even though it's absolutely, overwhelmingly there. You never want to give your child a reason to say to themselves, "Well, I'm never telling my mom (or dad) anything ever again." We want our children to always feel comfortable to come to us, especially about the serious and scary stuff. Don't get mad. Don't get frustrated. Don't act annoyed. Don't act as if you're sick of hearing it. Don't assume you know their reasoning. Don't assume anything.

Do ask questions. Empathize and validate your child's emotions. Reach out for help for your child and for yourself.

What to say

You may be thinking something like *How the hell am I going to talk to my kid about something so scary and dark? What if this puts it on the table for them?* Obviously, this is a scary topic. And how is a teenager going to understand it? Are they going to take what you say completely different from what you mean?

When is the right time to discuss suicidal ideation with your child? First off, I believe that being open and honest with your children, at any age, is important. One of the biggest indicators that it's time for this talk is when your child starts bringing it up. If you have developed a close connection with your child with an open and honest relationship, your child will come home and talk about all sorts of things with you. And sometimes that topic is suicide.

Start out by writing your goals for having the discussion. What exactly do you want for your child to take away from the discussion? Is your child young, a preteen, or already a teenager? It's best to always start conversations with a soft opening that includes your feelings and why you want to have this discussion. Sharing the goals that you made is a great way to open the discussion.

Young children

For young kids (5–10 years old), I suggest that you start by asking what they think suicide is or know about it. You can try something along the lines of "This is really hard for mommy to talk about because it is something that is sad. Sometimes, there are sad things that happen, and I want you to know that it's okay to talk about those with me. You asked me about suicide, and it took me a minute to figure out what to say to you. What do you think suicide is?" Actively listen to their response, and reflect on what you hear before continuing.

You can then continue: "Suicide is a very sad thing. You know how, when people get really old or really sick, they die? Do you remember what dying means?" Again, you should actively listen to their response and reflect what you hear before continuing.

"The thing about suicide is that it doesn't have to happen. Unlike some other ways that people die, this is one that we can make sure doesn't happen to us. Suicide is when someone is so sad, and maybe doesn't have a mommy or daddy to help them, that they choose to end their life. They find a way to die by making that choice. It can get a bit more complicated, so we can always talk more about this if you want. Does this make sense? Do you have any questions for me?"

Finally, make sure they understand: "What do you understand suicide to be now that we've talked?"

Preteens

Preteens (10–12 years old) have most likely heard the word *suicide* and have somewhat of an understanding of what it is. In today's culture, there's no doubt that it is a topic circling their social groups, whether they're paying attention or not.

You can start the discussion like this: "This is one of those times that I need to talk to you about an adult subject, but it is really hard for me to know exactly what to say. Since you're getting older, I want to have talks with you because I know you can handle them. I want you to know that no question is off limits, and I will try to explain to the best of my ability. It's important for us to talk about this because it is something that you're inevitably going to hear about, and I'd really like for you to know the correct information from me and know that this is something you can come to me about. What do you think suicide is?"

You should actively listen to their response and reflect what you hear before continuing.

"Suicide is one of those scary life things that can be really hard to talk about. Sometimes, life can feel really hard, and some people feel like giving up. It's a really sad place for someone to be. I'm sure you know some friends at school that seem down or sad most of the time. It's kind of like that but way worse. Or you know those times when you're having a bad day and you can't seem to feel better until you rest a little and start a new day? Some people don't feel better that quickly and struggle for a long time. It can be because they never learned how to handle tough situations, or maybe they struggle with a mental health illness like depression. Suicide is a choice that some people make when they can't seem to feel better. It is the wrong choice because there is always hope and ways to feel better. Sometimes, it takes a little practice, but when someone chooses to end their life, they are giving up and not thinking about the long-term effect. Think about all of the people who care about that person."

As with any age child, you want to follow up to make sure they know you're available for more discussion and to make sure they understand what you've discussed: "Does this make sense? Do you have any questions for me? What do you understand suicide to be now that we've talked?"

Teens

Junior high and high school teens have definitely heard the word *suicide*, they've been involved in conversations about it, and they know people who are sad a lot and some who aren't but still talk about it. They have friends who talk about it or share some pretty dark thoughts. They know numerous peers who have attempted it, and sadly, there is a good chance they have lost a classmate already. I suggest a conversation whether they bring it up or you do. Address the very dark and heavy elephant in our world. You could even start by mentioning this book; use it as an icebreaker. Remember your goals, and share those with your teen first.

- "I want to have an understanding of what you know suicide to be and looks like."
- "I want us to have a relationship that allows these types of discussions to happen because there will be more dark and heavy topics that come up in your future."

- "I want to get an idea of where you're at with this topic and how it may affect you."

- "This is an uncomfortable conversation for me. I have a lot of fear with this, but I trust that you and I can talk about this because you are entering adulthood."

Like many conversations with our kids that involve big topics, we need to expect to have multiple discussions. Your child will not absorb everything all at once. Check-ins with your child are important. Actively choosing to bring it up again is important. This is not a one-and-done conversation. Talking with your child about these topics will help them feel safe with you and will also keep you in tune with their thoughts on the subject. Talking about it with them will not encourage them to go do it. Some of your goals for talking to your child may include providing a place for them to talk and ask questions, helping them understand the scary aspects, for them to find fear in the topic, and to help them see what contributes to it in today's culture. This can help become a starting point to talk about some of the things you'd like to change that are currently in your family's lifestyle.

The smartphone

The smartphone is a wonderful tool that has turned into one of the scariest and most exhausting pieces of technology in our homes. It would be unrealistic to think we could eliminate technology, and it won't do any good to try. Once our kids are in elementary school, they begin using technology in class, and it continues from there. But is it possible to provide the emotional tools to avoid using technology as their coping skill? Is it possible to find balance between phone use and true face-to-face connection? Can we live in a world with both less immediate gratification and the convenience of technology? It is possible to limit their screen time while they are young, and when they are a bit older, teach them by gradually allowing more screen time and helping them understand the process.

There's a good chance your teenager is addicted to their phone. If your teenager can admit that they are addicted, they are ready to make some changes. Here's the thing though: It's really hard to admit something to your parents if there is any shame associated with it. Since you're likely struggling with the same addiction—or maybe you have struggled with something similar—this is something that can be addressed with an empathetic heart and understanding. Some validation would also be helpful here.

When I was in high school, I was addicted to AOL Instant Messenger. I didn't know it at the time, but looking back now, it's very clear. AIM was my lifeline to connecting with friends. It was very similar to what we know social media to look like today. I couldn't wait to rush home to see who was online and would stay on it for hours. I would stay up way too late, lose sleep, fight with my parents, and struggle through family time just to get back on the computer. Sounds familiar, huh? My parents knew I was obsessed. They would take it away from me when I didn't meet their expectations with chores, grades, or my attitude toward them. They would tell me that I had a problem. They voiced it, and I would get defensive.

My parents were concerned. They would say that I would be upset at first but then I was always much more pleasant to be around without it in my life. And they were right. But would I have ever admitted that to my parents? Hell, no! They would've given me the "told-you-so-see-we're-so-smart" lecture. I didn't want to admit that I was wrong or that I had a problem because I felt ashamed and alone. Although my parents didn't intend to make me feel that way, it was happening. Throw in some of my natural stubborn ways, and there was absolutely no way I would've surrendered.

I sit with teenagers daily who admit this same series of feelings to me. They agree with my concern, and they talk about their love/hate relationship with their phone. How do we help our child see that there is a problem? We join them in the problem. We allow the process of self-discovery and brainstorm solutions together so they don't feel like they have failed at life. This is one of those really hard parts.

At this point, it's not realistic to think you're just going to take away their access to their phone or social media. But here are some ideas:

My teenage clients both hate and love social media and technology, which tells me they are somewhat aware of the negative effects. While remembering not to shame or put down your teen for liking their phone too much or for their social media obsession, you can encourage an open discussion about it, allowing them to be honest. The moment there is any criticism or perceivable disappointment from you, your teen may feel an attack on their character or strength as an individual, and that will create a defensive tone. Your job is to simply listen and reflect what you hear your teenager express:

- "Tell me your thoughts on social media."
- "Do you think people spend too much time on their phones?"
- "What do you gain being on social media a lot?"
- "Is it possible for us to talk about some balance in your life?"

I wish I had felt comfortable to say to my parents when I was addicted to AIM, "I don't know how to handle it. And I'm not sure I *want* to handle it. Because I really do like it. I like talking to my friends and connecting with them. But it does consume most of my time, and I'm dealing with lack of sleep." That is not so much asking for help but more admitting that I agree with them. It is hard to agree with your parents when you have built an adversarial relationship.

I often hear from clients that there are times when they don't have their phone and it feels so good and freeing. One client went on a mission trip in Guatemala for a week and voiced how much she enjoyed sitting and reading a book without the concern of her phone. We can't take technology away—nor should we—but we can learn how to live with it without unhealthy effects.

We haven't felt the need to teach our kids what social media is intended for because we have been discovering and evolving with it ourselves. But now that we have seen the repercussions and have better understanding, it is time to take action. The Internet has always been a place that parents have been taught to warn their children against predators in chat rooms and forums. It has now reached a point that is impossible for a parent to truly monitor all that their child is seeing, hearing, and creating. There are too many platforms and loopholes. This world has gotten bigger than just an AOL chat room.

I'm also usually caught on the fence with the idea of parents going through their child's phone. To me, it's similar to a parent reading their child's diary or journal. There are times of true fear for your child when it is necessary. There are also times when parents do it out of curiosity or playing the game of "I'm gonna catch you! You think you're so sneaky!"— which, for the record, I don't agree with that reasoning.

Phone and Internet training

Just like training to drive, we need to train phone and Internet responsibility gradually. There is no age recommendation necessarily; it's important to take into account your child's maturity level, as well as your benefit from getting them a phone. Do you want to know where your child is? Do you want to have your child call you when they are done with band practice? Do you need to know that your child is safe while at their dad's for the weekend?

Once you are comfortable with your child having some responsibility and freedom, there are luckily many good options today. You can get them a flip phone or a kid's smartwatch. Be careful which one you choose; I would avoid the ones that allow games and multiple apps. You want to look for one that has GPS and can contact a select few phone numbers from the watch. You could also look into a walkie-talkie if your child will be staying in your neighborhood. There are also some GPS devices that have a walkie-talkie feature that connects to an app on your phone (not theirs).

Once your child grows and has become successful with the beginning steps of phone responsibility, it is time to discuss a more advanced option. Trust your gut. Go into this decision remembering what we've discussed about addiction, the negative effects of social media, and the inability to connect. You want them to understand this new responsibility and all that comes with it. Explain your expectations and the rules that you have decided on.

Suggested expectations and rules

- The device must be fully charged.
- Your child must share their passwords with you.
- They must leave the device downstairs in the charging zone overnight.
- You must have final approval of all app downloads.
- Social media accounts must not share location and must be set to private (for example, with Instagram, you can set whether strangers can see your pictures or whether they have to request to be your follower first).
- Any time that is meant for socializing or interacting with others, the phone is put away.

You'll also want to continue your conversation with them regarding various related topics: Starting out with their first phone, you want your child to be aware of your intention for them having their own phone.

Phones are intended for communication, not only playing games or social media. If you believe they are not ready for social media or they struggle with phone addiction playing games, it needs to be made clear that their phone is strictly for communication.

Teaching our teens how to be on social media can seem daunting and complicated. I believe that by starting the conversation before you allow them to have their own accounts—say, when they are 8 and see you scrolling through your own Facebook or Instagram feed—it will make the transition of handling it themselves much smoother. Remembering the five concerns social media presents, you can establish what you want your child to learn and what to avoid. Social media is intended for connecting with those whom you can't connect with face-to-face. It's important to have conversations with your child on the positive effects of confronting someone who has hurt them directly in person, rather than on social media. The expression of complex emotions on social media is ineffective. It creates a world of conflict and spreads the hurt faster than we can catch it. Instead, teach your children about all the hurt people on social media. Hurt people hurt people. They can choose to break the cycle and sometimes knowing why some people act the way they do, the sting doesn't hurt as bad.

Teach your child Internet intelligence. It can be a casual conversation that gets brought up throughout their childhood—a simple "There are things online that get sent to my email that after reading it, I can tell it's fake and someone is trying to trick me." We have to teach our kids stranger danger in a new way. What are the signs of someone who is tricky online? What would someone who is planning to be inappropriate say or do to lead your child to believe something and open up a relationship? What do "creepers" do to seem normal and friendly to kids?

As a parent, it's hard to keep up, but I strongly encourage you to invest time in understanding the different apps your child is into. You can set your phone to notify you for approval before your child can download an app. Get your own account on the apps that your child wants, not necessarily to keep tabs on them but to understand the ins and outs of what goes on with each app.

Set time limits for your child to use social media in the phone's settings. Some parents set it for an hour per day; some set it for three hours. Find what you are comfortable with, and once your child uses the time allotted, it won't allow them to be on it again in a 24-hour period. Teach them about time and place for looking through social media or using their phone, prioritizing face-to-face connection with family and friends and saving phone use for later.

Check out Bark. It is an app that helps monitor your child's phone. It filters text messages and social media messages, so you don't have to go through their phone.

Talk about what you are doing with other parents. If you are the only one who makes changes, it is going to make life very hard for your child. Others have to be on board and feel it is the best for their child's brain development.

All of this can be handled by being open and talking with our kids. When they're little, we can get on our phones and announce what we're doing. They don't know that you're checking the weather or reading an email. They don't know that you're looking at the maps to figure out what time you need to leave to make it to the birthday party. They just see you on the phone. If you announce what you're doing, it can help them understand what all we use our phones for.

Watch what you say and how it might be perceived by your child. If you are scrolling through Facebook or Instagram and you make a remark about what others are doing or you find yourself comparing too much, put it down. When you are with your child, be present. Save the scrolling through social media for when they are not around. That doesn't mean you spend every waking hour with your child, but don't let them ever feel that your phone is more important than they are.

Encourage Resilience

> "It's like I'm happy for a little bit but then I get sad again.
> I just don't understand why I can't just be happy. I'm so
> annoyed. And like I have nothing to do. I just think about
> how I don't want to be here anymore."
>
> —16-YEAR-OLD STRUGGLING WITH SUICIDAL THOUGHTS

t is necessary to be resilient in this hard life. You must be able to be strong. From getting out of bed after a long, sleepless night to fights with your spouse to pulling an all-nighter studying in college to working your ass off for that promotion you've had your eye on for more than a year to struggling through financial lows and making ends meet, life is hard. We are all stronger than we think we are, but when we doubt ourselves, it's much harder to find that strength. Resilience is a necessary survival mechanism, and it's part of our jobs as parents to prepare our kids for those really hard moments.

Emotional hurricanes

Hurricane Harvey spat devastation on Houston in 2017. As the hurricane approached, we were warned that it was going to be one of the worst storms Houston had ever seen. Many were told to evacuate their homes, and some were assured that it wouldn't affect them because their home wasn't in a flood zone. Everyone either paid attention to the warning signs and prepared or didn't think it would be bad at all and didn't prepare.

Those who prepared stocked up on water and canned goods. They rented generators should the power go out. They taped up and boarded their windows. They protected their belongings, pets, and children, and many chose to leave their homes behind. Those who prepared accepted that a hurricane was coming and did what needed to be done to physically prepare.

Those who didn't believe it would be bad or didn't imagine they would be affected sat around waiting for it to pass. Some had every right to think they wouldn't be affected. Areas that hadn't been flooded ever before were being told that they needed to evacuate. We've had some pretty horrible hurricanes in Houston, and certain areas have been told that they needed to prepare but then nothing happened, so it was easy to think, "Eh! We'll be fine! Let's get a deck of cards and some wine and bunk up!" For some, the biggest fear was getting cabin fever from staying inside for days.

Harvey came in fast and strong. It was a scary few days for everyone. If we weren't under mandatory evacuation, we were told not to leave our houses. All we had was what was available within our homes. We were unsure when it was going to be over. We didn't know what was truly around the corner. We were unaware of what others were going through or how bad it had gotten for some (until it was posted on social media, of course). It was out of our control.

As the skies became dark, the storm was overwhelming, unsettling, and then it started to flood. For some, water began to rise and destroy belongings. Possessions were being taken away right before their eyes. People had to be rescued by boat while standing on the top of their roofs. Doubtful feelings took over, and many felt defeated and exhausted and were left thinking, *How long will this last? How can we get through it? Are others dealing with this as bad as us?*

Many within our community were left without their belongings and overwhelmed with a to-do list that felt impossible. I had friends who had to move their families into their parents' houses. There were people I knew professionally, as well as personally, who were affected by the wipeout and left with nothing. That is, those who didn't prepare were left with nothing.

Those who had prepared their home for Harvey experienced it a little differently. Their skies still became dark and unsettling, but they knew they had what it took to get through. They questioned when it would end, but they knew the answer was that it would, in fact, end. It started to flood, and they were devastated knowing their possessions and homes were being destroyed—although less so than those who didn't prepare. Valuables secreted away in waterproof safes and storage units, homes blocked with sandbags were still damaged, but that damage was less devastating. Those who stockpiled water and food were still stuck in their homes—but they had the supplies they needed. They took the appropriate steps to protect what needed protection. They knew they could get through the experience.

Life is hard, remember? It is not always easy, and sometimes, it's downright horrible. When something bad happens or we find ourselves in a bad place, I like to call this an *emotional hurricane*. We feel flooded and dark. It's overwhelming, and we are unsure how long it will last. We question how we will get through it, and we become emotionally exhausted, drained, and defeated. And oftentimes we feel alone. A problem such as adjusting to a new routine can be overwhelming, as can a big fight with your spouse, your mom getting diagnosed with breast cancer, your child being filled with sass for the past week, divorce, or grieving the loss of a family member. Is it possible to prepare for emotional hurricanes so we get through them easier? We know they are going to happen; it's inevitable. Every life is a flood zone. So what can we do to make them easier?

Those who have accepted that emotional hurricanes happen prepare for them. They don't always know what kind of emotional hurricane is headed their way, but they find ways to prep for any kind of hurricane. They set up their emotions to go in strong and are able to handle the darkness and uncertainty with confidence that it won't last forever. They are able to manage with what they have and power through.

In order to teach our children strength and resiliency, we have to help them become aware of their experience with emotional hurricanes. Sometimes, when an emotional hurricane is coming, there are obvious warning signs. As a parent, we may be able to easily spot them and bring them to our child's attention. By allowing our children to discover their own warning signs and identify patterns within their lifestyle, the desire for personal improvement is stronger. This helps your child become self-aware of their sensitivities and stressors or triggers, so prepping for the hurricane is doable. However, sometimes, the hurricanes hit without any warning at all. How does someone prep for a crisis they had no idea was headed their way?

Handling an emotional hurricane is a three-step process.

1. Practice self-care regularly, not just when shit hits the fan.
2. Be aware of warning signs, and put your coping skills and distraction methods into play.
3. Accept that the hurricane has arrived, find a peaceful mantra, and power through it.

All hurricanes end. And if you follow these steps, it won't last as long or feel as intense.

Hurt people hurt people

Remember the movie *How the Grinch Stole Christmas*? How mean the Grinch was! His heart was two sizes too small, and he wanted to ruin Christmas for everyone. It turns out that he wanted to ruin Christmas because he never got to enjoy Christmas himself. When he was a little boy, an orphan, he didn't have a family to enjoy all the magic of Christmas. And then at the end of the story, little Cindy Lou Who opens her heart, her arms, and her home to him, and his heart grows by three sizes. He is no longer hurting. He is no longer trying to ruin Christmas for anyone. He is no longer mean. Hurt people hurt people.

There are many different forms of hurt. What if we showed people grace when they do something hurtful to us—even our kids? It doesn't necessarily take the pain away, but sometimes it can help make the sting less intense. And what if we start to look inward at some of our own actions that cause hurt in others so we can start to understand and take ownership of those actions?

All negative emotions are rooted in hurt. In the counseling field, anger is known as a secondary emotion to either fear or hurt. I believe in taking it a step forward: Fear is a secondary emotion to hurt as well, along with all other negative emotions. There are some emotions that we don't consider to be negative, but after you look at how we react to them or how we experience them, they too are forms of hurt.

Hurt may be in the form of:

- Fatigue

- Hunger

- Selfishness

- Jealousy

- Anger

- Fear

- Sadness

- Neglect

When one of my boys was 5, I got a phone call from his teacher that he had been involved in a situation at school. No one likes getting these calls. My heart fell into my stomach, and I felt queasy.

"Another student was having a bad day," the teacher said, "and your son got caught in her path while she was having a breakdown. He got stabbed with a pencil. He's okay though—just a little blood, and he's been in a good mood since it happened."

My first reaction was anger. Who was this little kid stabbing my son?! My second thought was, *Okay, I'm glad he's okay and that his mood wasn't affected.* When I picked him up that afternoon and asked him about his day, he didn't even mention it.

"Hey buddy! Anything exciting happen today?"

"Eh, no. I don't think so."

"I heard something happened with a pencil?"

"Oh! How'd you know about that? Yeah, Maddie got mad and took a pencil and just WHAM right into my heart, Mom! But she's just tired, Mom. You know how you say that when we don't sleep, we are grumpy and not so nice? I think she's just tired."

And that was it. He just blew it off. He didn't take it personally or hold a grudge. I was proud of his reaction and glad that it wasn't turned into this big traumatic event. He didn't see himself as a victim.

Mean people are horrible sometimes. But if we replace the word *mean* with *hurt*, it shifts the focus and our attitude toward them: Hurt people are horrible sometimes. Hurt people need help to stop hurting.

And attitudes are highly contagious. When my kids experience someone being mean to them, I try to help them look at the situation fully. Rather than only focusing on how horrible it was (after some validation of feelings first, of course), we discuss what might be going on in the other child's world that caused them to react this way. Are they not getting good sleep? Did they not eat a good breakfast? Does their mom not kiss them goodnight every night? Did my child provoke them or do something hurtful first?

Social media is the perfect setup for hurt people, so hurt people are on social media. And many of those hurt people love to use social media to hurt others. It is just too easy. They don't have to directly confront someone; they can hide behind a screen and not have to make eye contact or act tough or say a clever comeback on the spot. If hurt people hurt people then that *must* mean that hurt people can sometimes recognize their behavior, take ownership of their pain, and not spread it on. And if we can teach our children that there are a lot of hurt people in this world and to not allow it to spread to their hearts and then on to someone else, maybe we can stop some of the hurt more easily than we thought.

Finding opportunities to teach our kids how to become self-aware of hurt is the easy part; it's happening left and right. But what we really want is for our kids to become self-aware on their own. Starting at a young age, you can begin by verbalizing for them how they (probably) feel—that is, validate the emotion displayed. Also verbalizing your own hurt will model to your child how to appropriately express their feelings. If this is done consistently, as they mature emotionally, you will find that they begin to verbalize it to you before you get the chance. This is a huge success. Once they begin self-awareness, you can open up the conversation to find solutions or understanding for the hurt feeling. Remembering that hurt people hurt people, you can begin the discussion with your child about recognizing their hurt and not spreading it to another person.

For teenagers, so much of their identity is based on acceptance—by friends, by family, and today, of their digital self (social media). If you don't teach and remind your teen that hurt people hurt people, there is a strong chance that when—not if—they experience a hurtful person spreading hurt to them, they will begin to have dark, heavy, and scary thoughts. Cyberbullying or even an argument with a friend that gets out of hand can feel like the worst emotional hurricane. It's just too much. Opening up the conversation with them to understand that hurt people are hurting others—that this is one of the causes for the empty feeling they may have—can relieve some of the pain, change the perspective, and clear the storm.

Implement Emotional Hygiene

"If there was as much focus on our emotional balance as there is football and grades, our world would be so much better. Why is this not taught in school? Why do we all have to discover this on our own when we're old?"

—FATHER OF A 15-YEAR-OLD STRUGGLING WITH ANXIETY

Just like we all need personal hygiene, we all need emotional hygiene. Emotional hygiene is the act of prioritizing emotional self-awareness to nurture our own mental health. Once we prioritize our emotional and mental health, we are able to figure out what works to keep ourselves centered and balanced. If we teach our children how to establish some of their basic emotional needs alongside their basic physical needs while they're young, we are setting them up for success to be a well-rounded human being.

First, we have to understand what emotional hygiene entails. After that has been evaluated and discovered by asking yourself the following questions, you can look at what you need and how you can achieve those needs to then teach your kids. You deserve healthy emotional hygiene, as does every member of your family.

- What does self-care look like?

- What can you add to your life that is good for you?

- What can you commit to routinely that will bring your life emotional ease?

- How much sleep are you getting, and what does your diet look like?

- Does your life feel balanced or overwhelmingly imbalanced?

Self-care

Self-care is the foundation of productive emotional hygiene. As parents who practice self-care, we also need to teach our children self-care. It comes in four main forms:

- Physical (sleep, exercise, healthy food, personal hygiene)

- Emotional (stress management, self-awareness, compassion, kindness, emotional maturity)

- Social (boundaries, support systems, healthy social media practice, communication, relationships)

- Spiritual (alone time, ways to recharge, religion or meditation, personal connection)

Typically, we wait for something horrible to happen to calm our bodies and minds. What if we practiced activities or coping skills that kept us centered and calm on a more frequent basis? This can help us prepare for those unexpected hurricanes. If you know a hurricane is coming, that's a good time to increase your self-care a bit. If you practice some form of self-care regularly, what you're really doing is strengthening your emotional stability. Taking bubble baths shouldn't be held only for a bad day; maybe add it to your routine to create balance between stress and relaxation.

This does not mean that the hard times won't be hard. They will. But you won't feel as dark, flooded, overwhelmed, out of control, unsure, defeated, or exhausted. Rather, you will feel upset and sad but also strong and confident enough to power through the struggle. The goal here is to figure out what you need as an individual so you can be the best possible version of yourself. And that best version of you will spread to your role as spouse, parent, friend, sibling, coworker, and any other hat you wear daily.

If you are a social butterfly but you're stuck at home drowning in housework, you're going to feel imbalanced. And that imbalance is going to affect how you feel about yourself and how you treat others. It's a domino effect that can create more problems. If we don't prioritize self-care, we fall into a sinkhole, and it feels impossible to get out. If you know that you are someone who needs to be outside—whether that's doing something athletic or just feeling the fresh air—but you're stuck inside trying to stay on top of things, you're going to feel repressed. You're going to feel that your life is deprived of something. You aren't going to feel complete. And that will bleed into other areas of your life; it will all be affected.

So if you know these things about yourself, it's time to prioritize yourself just a little bit. Don't take it to the extreme; that would be selfish. But concentrate on it so you are balanced, and therefore, other areas of your life can excel and benefit from that balance. We all need a portion from each of the four types. Evaluate yourself and how much you need from each to achieve that balance and combination that helps you the most. Just as if you are diabetic or anemic, take what your body is deprived of, take that medicine so you are balanced, and get on with it. You won't be able to function properly without it. That is self-care.

Avoiding selfishness

It is fair to ask yourself, *But isn't it selfish of me to take time out of the day to do what I want to do?* This can get very confusing for young minds, so it is important to distinguish the difference between self-care and being selfish. And since selfishness is not a characteristic we wish for our children (it is not part of your parenting philosophy), we must help them understand how to recognize the difference.

It all depends on one thing: consideration. If you make all of your self-care needs decisions based solely on yourself and what you want to do at that moment without taking others into consideration, you're being selfish. We have to be careful not to do something selfish by justifying it and convincing ourselves that it's self-care. Many of us are guilty of doing this.

For example, if you and a good friend go shopping because you want to splurge and treat yourself—a little retail therapy, if you will—and you have specific stores that you want to hit up, great. But if you go and never once ask your friend where they would like to go or if they need to shop anywhere in particular and only go where you want, that's selfish. If you go and share that you really want to make sure you go to Nordstrom and find that they want to go there, as well as Francesca's, and you make time for all of it, it falls in the self-care category. You're getting your retail therapy while considering who you are with.

If you lack balance in your life and need to set aside time for you to center yourself because you're about to lose your effing mind, that is truly self-care. Training your brain, working out, or—if you like my phrase— emotional hygiene, whatever you want to call it, you are concentrating on how to be the best version of yourself *with* the consideration of those you care about in your life.

Balance

I have said it before, and I will say it over and over and over again for the rest of my life: *Balance is necessary*, in every aspect of our lives. If you eat a piece of cake, you need to balance it with an apple. If you say something mean to someone, you need to balance it with something kind. If you take something from someone (even if they offer it), you need to balance it by giving to another. If you have a negative thought, balance with a positive one. If you hate something about yourself, you need to love something about yourself. If your child spends four hours gaming, they need to spend four hours not gaming. If you isolate from your family and friends, you need to immerse yourself in a social setting. If your child spends hours studying or working on homework, they need to balance with relaxation or play. If you spend hours working out, you need hours of rest or time spent working toward something else. If you spend a lot of time with a certain person, you need to balance it with time with others or spent alone. If you watch a scary movie, you need to watch a Disney movie next. Balance is key.

I encourage you to look at your daily lifestyle. How much balance is there? What about your child's life? How much balance are they receiving? What can you do to make this change for your family?

As our society has embraced such a fast-paced lifestyle, almost nobody prioritizes balance. Therefore, our kids aren't able to witness it or value it. It's as if it's a way of life, and instead of figuring out how to make things more stable or less hard (notice I didn't say *easy*), we pile more and more on. We avoid balance and the acceptance of reality: There are just not enough hours in the day to cram it all in, but we keep pushing it and expect a different result, wearing ourselves down to nothing. And so are our kids.

Look at yourself now. Hopefully you can confidently look at yourself and say, "Nope, Tessa. I'm not one of those people. I have accepted myself and have found the balance needed for a smoother lifestyle." Bravo. Please join me in helping others reach that. But I am certain that most of you can't genuinely do that. And I'd like to encourage you to find the balance that will get you closer to a more comfortable lifestyle.

Here are some examples of self-care that I find are well received:

- Personal hygiene (showers, teeth brushing)
- Physical health (doctor appointments, healthy diet)
- Meditation
- Exercise
- Reading
- Sleep
- Therapy
- Socializing with those that bring positivity
- Church
- Volunteering
- Being outdoors
- Projects

I'd like to share my personal self-care list. Some activities are performed a few times a month, and some I prioritize daily. It all depends on what my balance scale looks like and what I feel I need to bring it back to a balanced center.

- House projects that teach me a new skill and I feel extremely productive and proud for accomplishing
- Getting my hair done (if you know me, you know why this is one)
- Quality time with my husband

- One-on-one time with one of my kiddos

- Journaling or writing

- Coffee or lunch with a girlfriend

- Going to Target

- Sleep

- Therapy

- Bubble baths

- Photography

- Puzzles and coffee

- Singing or listening to music

- Watching a favorite movie

What is on your list? Once you've created your self-care list, you can begin focusing on what you need to feel balanced: how much sleep you need a night, what your marriage needs to feel safe, what household chores you need to prioritize and which ones you can leave for the next day, which friends to make time for, and how much work is too much.

Next, you can sit down with your kids and let them make a self-care list too. But don't do it for them. They need to be encouraged to come up with their own list. Let them be in control of this one. As long as they can talk, they can come up with their own list. You may need to brainstorm a little with them, but they've got this.

Here are some questions to ask your child to get their brain thinking:

- What do you like to do for fun?

- What do you like to do that is relaxing?

- What can you do to feel better when you're in a bad mood?

This is my oldest son's self-care list:

- Play with LEGOs
- Ride my bike
- Jump on the trampoline
- Play video games
- Watch a movie with Mom
- Go on a walk
- Have a dance party
- Play with friends
- Collect Pokémon cards

Sometimes, life is going to throw something at us that creates imbalance. Even if we are extremely good at keeping the balance, it could be an emotional hurricane or just an extra errand or a project that got forgotten about until the night before. There are times we may need to make an exception that keeps us from practicing our emotional hygiene self-care list fully. Exceptions are completely okay. Sometimes they are necessary. But we can't let it create an imbalance for too long. Understanding that it has thrown things off will help you adjust back to center.

Sleep hygiene

Sleep might be the number-one complaint I hear from my clients, no matter the age. Although there are studies[8] and professionals who constantly give this advice, it still seems to be a mystery to so many.

At the young age of 20, I was like many others who struggle with

---

8   National Sleep Foundation, https://www.sleepfoundation.org.

achieving a good night's rest. I was unaware of how to get good sleep and didn't feel I had anyone to turn to. My world was spiraling into a dark place—all because I wasn't sleeping. I noticed a pattern of thoughts that would circle through my head every evening when I would try to sleep—past mistakes, traumatic memories, guilt, and self-loathing. I just wanted to turn off my brain so I could go to sleep. I was desperate.

According to the National Sleep Foundation, a lack of sleep affects our overall physical and mental health.[9] Sleep affects our entire body, from how we physically feel to our emotions, our hormones, stress levels, and even our digestive system. It's powerful. We all are so tired, and so many of us claim to *love* sleep, yet very few of us prioritize it. Hurt people hurt people, right? Tired people are certainly hurt; that's why they're so grumpy. And there's a good chance that it is a factor in your child's or teen's grumpiness. The question isn't whether any of us *want* sleep but, rather, how we remember to prioritize sleep and fit it into our busy world.

Children and teenagers are recommended to get 10–12 hours of sleep in a 24-hour period. Adults are recommended to get 8–10. Without the proper amount of sleep, which seems nearly impossible to achieve, all those hormonal, stressful emotions are heightened and overwhelming. The lack of sleep might be the number-one reason people struggle with their emotions on a day-to-day basis.

Prioritizing sleep looks like this:

- Set a time that you'd like to fall asleep each night. Dare I call it a bedtime?

- Create a bedtime ritual or routine—washing your face, brushing your teeth, reading a book. Find what relaxes you before bed that you can consistently do, and do it.

---

9   "How Sleep Affects Your Immunity." National Sleep Foundation. https://www.sleepfoundation.org/articles/how-sleep-affects-your-immunity.

- Turn off the TV, even if you're really into a show. Your show will still be available tomorrow. Honor your bedtime.

- No phone or smart device for at least an hour before your goal bedtime. The blue light of your device's screen prevents your brain from releasing melatonin, which triggers sleepiness.

- Know that our thoughts will also still be there tomorrow, and we can deal with them when we're awake and have a well-rested brain. Make a list of things you want to think about tomorrow if you feel you may forget.

- List mentally or write out three things you're grateful for. It can be the Starbucks coffee you had this morning or the family you feel connected to. It will end your day on a positive note.

- Practice thought stopping

Thought stopping is consciously taking control of your thoughts by not thinking of what you're naturally thinking about but, rather, choosing a thought that you actually *want* to think about. Remember that part in *The Sound of Music* when Julie Andrews sings about her favorite things? When she's scared, she just closes her eyes and thinks of raindrops on roses and whiskers on kittens. That is Fraulein Maria's thought stopping in action.

Here's the bad news: Thought stopping is hard! It takes multiple times to really get this technique down. But if you're stubborn and determined like me, you can do it. It takes multiple times because you're *training* your brain. And like anything you train for, it takes practice and determination. The determination needs to come from the desire to prioritize sleep.

First, think of a thought that brings you comfort. This will be your default thought. It can be a fantasy, a memory, a prayer, a song, or simply imagining yourself at the beach. In order for thought stopping to work, you must have your default thought ready to go. You don't want to lie down and *then* think of it. You must also know that your default thought will most likely need to change throughout your life. One of mine used to be imagining my wedding day, and then I got married and it no longer became something for me to imagine. I had to search for something new to give me comfort. It is best to have two or three at hand in case one stops working.

The process for thought stopping looks like this:

1. You have a bad, anxious, sad thought.

2. You are self-aware that you're not falling asleep.

3. But you choose to prioritize sleep.

4. STOP!

5. Find your default thought.

6. Negative thoughts will inevitably creep back in.

7. Repeat steps 2–7 until you finally drift to sleep.

The good news is that if you get really good at this, you won't have to tell yourself to stop anymore. You'll get to a point that you automatically think of your comforting thought. It becomes the new natural. You'll have successfully trained your brain.

Depending on the age of your child, you can sit with them to come up with their default thought. Let them be creative. One night, when one of my boys couldn't sleep, he was having a nightmare (ahem, anxiety), so we sat there for a while trying to come up with something that would calm him and keep his mind occupied so he could drift to sleep. We named this his "Sleep Time Story." What you're really searching for is a comforting distraction so you can ease your mind and fall asleep. He ended up imagining himself flying with a dragon and going all over the world. Your child may need a song that brings them comfort. Or even go further, and they can imagine themselves performing that song in front of all their friends with the coolest outfit on. Sometimes, remembering a happy memory or thinking about an upcoming event works well too.

We want what's best for our kids, obviously, so we want them to feel good physically, emotionally, and hormonally; to experience low stress; and to have a strong digestive system. As I said, children and teenagers need 10–12 hours of sleep for the healthiest brain development, and getting that much sleep isn't really possible if they are studying, involved in sports or extracurriculars, and want to keep up with their social life and connect with the family. So how can we do this? I mentioned that teenage years are similar to toddler years. My kids are fresh out of the toddler years, so I remember it well. Their schedule and routine were based around sleep. Naptime and bedtime were the goals each day. Although academics, sports, social life, and family connections are very important, sleep needs to go to the top of the list. If our kids can get better sleep, they will naturally excel in all the other areas of their life. And you'll get better sleep too!

Beware of the dark side

One more note on self-care and sleep. Sometimes we need "a day." You know what I mean. We need to check out of reality. We need a day to veg out. Sometimes we need a moment to cry, eat a tub of ice cream, binge watch some trashy TV, and allow ourselves to be lazy. Especially in this world of *Go! Go! Go!*, we've got to balance that with some *No! No! No!* If this is something *you* need, then your child needs it too. It relieves the pressure and recharges the batteries.

However, this can get tricky. While vegging out can be good to help us rest, recharge, and even motivate, it can also go on too long, crossing us over to the dark side. What is too long for you? Everyone is different.

Your amount is most likely going to be different from your child's. It's going to take some experimenting. Is just the morning enough? Is one full day good? Do you need two days? If you can observe when you start to cross over—when relaxation turns to anxiety, sadness, heightened laziness, a lack of motivation, a lack of hygiene—and know your boundary, you'll be golden when you allow for these mental health days. But if you let it go on until you've already crossed over, you've now created imbalance, and you likely won't benefit from the rest at all. And why do anything that you can't benefit from? If you allow yourself to cross over, then you've just wasted all that really good veg time for nothing.

My crossover used to be after one full day; now I can't go more than four or so hours before feeling like a complete pile of doodoo, so I only allow myself a good three hours or less to truly veg out and relax. Learn what you need, and pick up on the signs that the cross over is near. Help your child by having discussions about how they feel after they rest. Then take that, and prevent them crossing over by creating a boundary.

Instill Coping Skills

"It was amazing. It was as if something so simple made me totally okay with everything. And all I did was start punching the punching bag anytime I'd get mad about anything. I haven't cut in weeks because of it. And I kinda feel badass when I'm doing it too!"

—18-YEAR-OLD STRUGGLING WITH DEPRESSION, ANXIETY, SUICIDAL THOUGHTS, AND SELF-HARM

As parents, we want to protect and provide for our children and also be tough on them, to teach them lessons, so they become strong, independent individuals. But it seems we have some of it backward. We are protecting them when we need to allow them to struggle and being tough on them when that may be harmful. For example, we often protect our children in social situations, to avoid their feeling hurt and left out, but we are tough on them when they are exhausted and having trouble managing their emotions.

Be a supporter

Men are often known as taking on the role of "fixer." How many times have women gone to their husband to vent about their day or share how stressed things have gotten at work (or home), and the husband then comes back with, "You know what you should do . . ."? I don't know about you, but when this happens with my husband, I instantly think, *No! I wasn't asking for help. I just wanted to cry to you or have you hold me!* Sometimes, I go further and think, *What—do you think I haven't thought of that already? You think I'm stupid?* Most of the time, women don't need a fixer; they need a listening ear. And so do kids.

As parents, we take on that same role of "fixer." We want to fix every problem our child is faced with. We don't want them to hurt or struggle. It hurts us to witness any kind of pain that they may be experiencing. And although they were once itty bitty and we had to fix everything, I see parents across the board nowadays not able to allow their child to build resilience and figure things out for themselves.

We need to allow our children to struggle. We have to allow them to go through the process of defeat, rejection, failure, and disappointment in order to build that emotional strength that is necessary to get through this hard life. We have to trust that there is a strength within them that they will discover and explore.

We put so much emphasis on academics and appearance but ignore emotional growth and life skills. We reprimand our children for bad choices and bad grades but aren't as concerned with how they get along with their friends or what is going on within them emotionally.

Allow the boredom. Allow the sadness. Let them realize that these feelings are temporary and that relief will come. When they are young, allow them to express feelings that are hard for their age. Allow them to experience this hard life as they are developmentally and naturally meant to. Drama with friends, school stressors, nightmares, feelings of confusion—allow it. Don't ignore it or minimize it. Rather, offer a listening ear. And if (and probably when) they ask for your guidance and thoughts, offer with the focus on the end goal—relief and strength. There will be moments when life is harder than usual for your child, and it is your job to gear them up for those exceptionally hard times.

A healthy relationship as a supportive parent should change over time—from a fixer when they are babies to a helper when they are nearing adulthood. A healthy relationship with our child has us gradually progress from the fixer role to the supportive role. We want to send our kids off into the world as fixers of their own life struggles, and as their supporters, we are on the sidelines, cheering them on while offering a helping hand (but not giving them all the answers).

However, parents often tend to get confused with their role and fail to execute a smooth transition from fixer to helper. When you feel yourself trying to fix your child's problem instead of listening and letting them figure it out, stop. Back up, and readjust your focus. Now, listen to what your child is saying, affirm it, offer help, and watch them grow as they learn how to figure out life's problems for themselves.

Coping skills

We all feel the feels from time to time. When you sense the warning signs, it's time to break out the coping skills. This is a little different from self-care but can look very similar; the difference is that you're using them for a distraction or to feel better because you're not feeling so great. Self-care options are supposed to happen whether you feel great or horrible. Coping skills help you get though the horrible times.

The hardest part of finding what coping skills work best for you is being self-aware. You have to build self-awareness of how you feel, how something affected your emotions, and how you react to that situation. Like any skill, you have to practice self-awareness to get good at it and to find what works best for you. It's our job to teach our kids how to become self-aware masters starting at a young age, and we can't do that if we struggle with it ourselves.

The Turnaround

When my oldest son was 4, he was pouting on the stairs, really mad at me, because I put his socks on for him and they were blue, not red. My "sweet" 4-year-old was throwing a fit over the color of socks he has on while I also tried to handle a second toddler and infant twins. Since I'm a big believer that attitudes are contagious, when it comes to something so silly, I don't tolerate an attitude from my kids. I was horrified that this negativity and tantrum throwing was going to spread like the plague. I could feel it growing within me, and I knew the other three kids wouldn't be far behind. So I looked at him with my very stern mom face, paired with the best mom voice I had, and said, "If you don't turn that attitude around right now, we're not meeting up with friends to play today."

What happened next was amazing. My sweet, curly headed 4-year-old looked at me with the meanest mug a cutie could give and swiftly turned his body around 360 degrees. When his face came back around, he had a big smile on his face.

I instantly started laughing, which made him laugh. At that moment, my 4-year-old taught me that, sometimes—not all the times, but sometimes—it's as easy as turning your attitude around, literally. I made him aware of his attitude, and he did something about it. At that age, kids need help becoming aware.

That moment goes down in our family history of the day he created a coping skill that my family now practices routinely. In our house, it has a 100% success rate. We call this The Turnaround, and we call each other out all the time. If someone is in a grumpy mood, you will often hear someone else say, "Looks as if you need a good turnaround!" If I ever send my boys to their room to cool down, I always follow with "Let me know when you're ready for a turnaround, and I'll do one with you." I call my husband out on it. The kids call us out on it. It really is helpful. It's a helpful reminder to become aware of how you're feeling and how you're acting.

Create a coping skills list

I have a lot of clients who hate the words *coping skills*, so I try to keep it out of my vocabulary. They're annoyed with it because they've either been hospitalized or through enough therapy that it's been branded as the "cure-all" answer that they need to discover, and either they don't want to or nothing has worked. There is no cure-all answer.

They also get upset because, for most of today's youth, their smartphone is their coping skill. Most of the time, parents don't like to hear this, especially when they punish by taking that technology away, but it's true. Coping skills are anything used to relax, soothe, or distract from bad thoughts or emotions. However, for adolescents, their phone has become their *only* coping skill that is actually causing many more problems.

I encourage all parents to sit with their child and help make a list of coping skills. Do not choose to do this in a moment of conflict or crisis. Rather, pick a calm environment and time to simply ask the question, *What do you do to make yourself feel better when you're feeling upset or sad?* See how they respond. I encourage writing the list out.

The child should be in control of this part; you're just there to help. However, if they truly are stumped, it's okay to brainstorm with them. Some popular coping skills in our house are:

- Alone time
- The Turnaround
- Playing outside
- Reading a book
- Helping others
- Punching a pillow
- Crying and hugging Mom
- Snuggling and talking
- Taking a bath
- Jumping on the trampoline
- Calling a friend
- Singing a song
- Listening to favorite music
- Coloring or drawing
- Playing the ukulele
- Riding a bike

The good thing about this list is that it's actually some good options for adults as well. Notice that many of these options can end up on your child's self-care list or may look very similar. My son uses the same list for both. That's okay, as long as self-care and coping are distinguished for separate needs. Self-care builds preparation against emotional hurricanes and provides balance, whereas coping skills help you feel better *during* the emotional hurricane.

When it comes down to it, we've got to help our kids build these skills and tools so when life gets tough, which it will, and they experience some real stress, which they will, they already know what works for them. If they wait until they're 12 or 13 to experience a sucky life and *then* try to find something that helps, it's going to be harder. It's never too late; it's just easier if it's been practiced for a bit before the emotional hurricane hits land.

Keeping busy versus distraction

It's good to keep busy when you're going through a tough time. Staying busy and distractions are not the same thing, and this can get a bit confusing. Keeping busy is making the choice to not focus or dwell on a negative thought or emotion. Keeping busy can lighten the load of negativity by helping you stay occupied with something productive. Distractions, on the other hand, are good to contribute to keeping busy, as well as getting through an intense emotional hurricane. However, distractions are more often used to completely avoid the problem at hand, brushing it under the rug and hoping it never surfaces. Spoiler alert: It always comes to the surface one way or another. There is an undeniable theme that comes along with most of the contributing cultural factors of this: smart devices. Finding something that completely distracts you, like using the phone for a coping skill, providing instant "relief," actually prolongs true relief and recovery.

Here is a story I share with my clients to help explain the need for distractions:

The haunted house

I hate horror films. I really tried to like them. I remember as a teenager forcing myself to go see the newest horror film with friends because everyone thought they were so cool. I hated every minute of it. Then I dated Carson, and he loved scary movies.

"Aw, you're so cute," he would say to me on those Friday nights at the movies. "Don't worry. I'll protect you."

I liked the idea of someone thinking I was cute and needed "protection," so I snuggled up close and struggled through the two hours of the movie. I still hated it.

So it would be confusing to many—including myself—why, at the age of 19, I thought experiencing a haunted house would be a good idea. Maybe I was open to trying new things and thought *Now that I'm older, I can handle it*, or maybe I just didn't want to be the only one waiting outside while my friends went in. I'm not sure, but it's very clear now that it was a bad idea.

Walking into the haunted house, my stomach started to turn. Actually, let me back up. Buying the tickets to go in, my stomach began to turn. Nope, even further back. The moment someone had the idea that we should go to a haunted house and the entire car full of friends all agreed with smiles and excitement, my stomach began to turn.

Why were they all so excited about this? Why was I the only one feeling uncomfortable and the only one who didn't actually *enjoy* getting scared? Although I was experiencing some anxiety, I put a smile on my face and decided that I could handle it. I knew it was all fake, and since I had never experienced a haunted house before, I told myself that I needed to live a little, lighten up, and try some new things. So I suppressed my anxiety by telling myself that it was going to be fine and that I might even like it.

Stepping into the haunted house, I was sandwiched between my very tall friends Adam and Bryan. I grabbed the back of Adam's shirt, although he was probably the most excited of them all. It was dark. I couldn't see much but could hear a lot. I couldn't see beyond the room we were currently in. I had no idea how long I was going to be in this house. There was no exit in sight.

Everyone experiences anxiety in their own way. I experience mine like bad butterflies in my stomach fluttering around, tightness in my chest, and the inability to take a full, deep breath. My stomach was turning worse than ever before, and no matter how hard I tried to remind myself that it was fake, nothing seemed to make me feel better.

I began breathing harder and faster. I began searching for any way to escape this real-life nightmare. But because it was dark and I was confined to one room, sandwiched between much taller people, my vision was limited. It was so dark, and with the random fog throughout, all I could see were the laces to my shoes. I began to cry. I had made everyone believe that I wanted to be there, and now I couldn't get out.

At some point, my feet stopped moving forward. Adam, because he was much bigger than me, kept walking—and jumping each time he was startled—and I lost my hold on his shirt. Now there was space in front of me but many people behind me screaming and jumping around, heightening my fear and anxiety. People started to push and yell, because I needed to keep moving forward. They were getting mad at me, but I couldn't move. I knew that if I kept moving forward, I would have to face more darkness and scary visuals. I was frozen.

Then I realized that staying frozen would keep me in there longer. I was stuck in the darkness. There was no good option. I could move forward and continue to be scared, or I could stay put and continue to be scared. I felt trapped. I quickly learned that the actors in the house prey on the weak and purposely target them. A freaky clown was walking toward me with a chainsaw.

I decided the better option was to power through. I couldn't collapse because I would be stuck with the clown. I started to remind myself that there was, in fact, an exit and that I just needed to get there. *This is temporary. I will get through this.* I started to sing *The Little Mermaid*'s, "Part of Your World" as loudly as I could to drown out all the noise. I placed my hands over my ears, squinted my eyes as much as I could without closing them completely, and quickly rushed to catch up to Adam. Before I knew it, I saw the exit sign and, with no hesitation, slammed my entire body on the door to escape that haunted house.

I was free. I could breathe again. People were laughing and talking about what part freaked them out the most. I was smiling, knowing that I was safe and that I had learned my lesson on haunted houses. I tried it. I didn't like it. But I got through it.

Sometimes, our anxiety takes over, and we're stuck in a dark place. Sometimes, dark thoughts overwhelm us, and we can't think clearly. We have two options. We can stay put and allow the thoughts and darkness to continue to be present, or we can push through by searching for the exit, knowing the darkness is temporary, and do whatever it takes to get there—like sing a song and plug up our ears to drown out the noise.

Boredom can be a good thing

My number-one rule is no smart device should be used during a time of boredom or distress. For children, I encourage boredom. Allow your child to be bored, even at the doctor's office. Boredom is a good challenge when your child is young. It allows their creative brains to be built and put to use. Practice becoming a supporter rather than a fixer by allowing them to struggle emotionally without technology. They will get through it. It's going to be hard at first. They are going to fight back, throw a fit, make a statement, feel it's unfair. And it is because it's taking away what they have used to combat boredom. And boredom sucks. But it is going to prevent intense and dangerous boredom for them when they are older.

For teenagers (and adults), boredom can be dangerous. This is when minds can get creative, but frequently, it's destructive ideas that pop up because of hurtful emotions they may be experiencing. Rather than "What can I do for myself that is good for me?" it is more like, "Fuck this life. I want something exciting/something different/instant relief, and I'll do anything to get it." While they are little, we can teach our children to handle boredom appropriately. If they are older, it is harder.

Balance is never achieved if someone is always staring at their phone. As the parent, it is your job to help create balance when it comes to your child's phone usage. There will be times when they don't have it—like at 2:00 a.m., when they should be sleeping—and they won't be able to turn to their phone.

Here are some questions to ask your teen to help them address boredom without using a phone:

- What are some things that you do to feel better when you're feeling low?
- What are some things you do when you don't have your phone?
- What are some things you think would help that maybe you've never tried before?
- What can you do when everyone else is busy or it's late at night and you are unable to do some of those coping skills? (Help your teen think of specific scenarios so there are backup plans.)

This also means that, as parents, we can't use our own phone as a boredom tool either. Become aware of how much you turn to your phone while waiting—at a red light, at the doctor's office, around the house waiting for the clothes to dry, or for someone to call you back. Find your balance so it isn't your boredom cure-all as well.

The "I'm bored" game

During a time of boredom, my two oldest created a simple game that helps them become distracted, stay busy, and pick something off their coping skills list. What started as a little LEGO spinner, similar to a spinning top, has now been transformed into a poster board with an arrow spinner to flick to find an option. It looks something like this (see the illustration) but much larger and on poster board:

I'M BORED

LEGOS · Play Outside · Read · Make Something for Mom · Dance Party

Similarly, we discovered this works as the "I'm Sad" game as well:

Instilling patience

Patience is a learned behavior, which means, even if we do a good job teaching our children when they're little how to be patient, once they get some instant gratification in their day-to-day lifestyle, that patience can be quickly unlearned. Try to slow down time a little. Helping your child find that balance between phone/technology use and other coping skills will teach them how to practice patience and build resilience.

While they are little, we are in control of how quickly they receive their satisfaction. Can we find some routine ways to create delayed gratification? Perhaps not allowing them to rent a movie just because they want to or not ordering everything through Amazon Prime, but rather regular shipping, would show them that not everything must happen now, now, now.

When going through a tough time or after having a bad day, instant gratification can feel satisfying, but, as I mentioned before, it only prolongs the true relief necessary to gain insight. Instant relief doesn't actually provide true relief. The minute the phone is taken away, the problem is back—and stronger. Using the phone to feel better works, but it distracts so much that thoughts can't be processed or worked through. Staying busy is good. Distractions are not. Grab that coping skills list and encourage your child to pick one!

12

Wait for Emotional Maturity

"I really think my ability to become self-aware was what I needed to get through this. That and therapy!"

—KINSLEY, 18-YEAR-OLD NO LONGER STRUGGLING WITH SELF-HARM OR SUICIDAL THOUGHTS

Emotional maturity is a natural, ongoing journey for each individual. Each of us is always growing, learning, maturing, and looking for understanding and acceptance; it's all part of being human. We all have our story and moments in our life that stand out to contribute to that emotional maturity.

Our kids experience their own journey and growth daily. This helps them prepare and power through emotional hurricanes, build resilience, and experience self-awareness to avoid dark and scary thoughts. Emotional maturity is, as you know, a combination of multiple factors and experiences. As parents, we take on the role of encouraging, teaching, supporting, and building our child's motivation to continue growing. Self-awareness, acceptance, and purpose within their life, particularly during a trying season, are the main parts to building that emotional maturity.

The self

Now that you understand your frosted glass and the need to avoid fear-based parenting and have your parenting philosophy in place, you can help encourage your child to focus on their emotional maturity through self-awareness, self-trust, and self-regulation.

Encouraging self-awareness

Young kids need your help becoming self-aware. Without the ability to become self-aware, communication, conflicts, and emotions will be hard to manage for the remainder of their hard life. And their hard life will more likely be a hard-bad life rather than that hard-good life we want for them.

While they are young, you can help them by picking up on the warning signs of an oncoming emotional hurricane and bring it to their attention with a simple code word or sound. One of my boys struggles with recognizing his anger. He gets frustrated with himself or frustrated with his brothers, and that can potentially turn into a screaming, crying fit. Instead of me interfering *after* he hits his brother with "You need to learn that we don't hit," I've learned to catch it beforehand. I've picked up on some words he says or sounds (whining) he makes when he starts to feel this way, and I bring it to his attention. A simple "Hey, buddy. This is one of those times." Or even just an "Uppuppuppuppup" mom sound, and he's learned to notice it, reflect, and gain some control. I've noticed I have to do it less often over time; he's starting to learn to become self-aware on his own and to gain some strength.

Older kids are much more aware of their emotions but may not know what to do with them. Teach them how to ask some questions. This will begin the process of self-reflection and the ability to pick up on warning signs on their own before the emotion becomes too overwhelming to handle:

- How do I feel in certain situations?

- Why did I have that reaction?

- What was my part?

- What was my intention?

- How could I have handled it differently?

Encouraging self-trust

When my boys were little and one would fall, I would quickly say, "You're okay! Get on up! Don't cry." I suppose it was part of that societal standard that boys have to be tough and not show emotion. Or maybe it was to just quickly remove my own discomfort. As parents, we too must practice self-awareness to understand whether minimizing our child's discomfort is really to minimize our own. Whatever the reason, I realized something: Telling them that they're okay, when they don't actually feel okay, is teaching them to mistrust themselves. If, every time you felt sick or stressed, someone said to you, "Oh, you're okay!" how would you react? I would feel dismissed, unimportant, cumbersome, and unheard. I might even feel the need to respond, "No, I'm not! What do you know about what I'm feeling?" and if I was younger, I might even feel the need to prove it more.

We want to teach our kids to be strong and to not coddle or enable them (which goes back to resilience). As I mentioned before, emotional hurricanes are going to hit their shore. Recognizing the storm is not weakening your child but, rather, encouraging them to struggle through instead of pretending it isn't there. This is an opportunity to teach rather than to minimize—or dictate—how they feel.

Children look up to their parents. They trust us. If we don't trust their sense of self and emotions, they begin learning to not trust themselves as well. Now, certainly, kids (and teenagers) can be dramatic. That doesn't necessarily mean they aren't hurting. Try to resist the, "Oh, you're okay!" statements, and instead respond with concern and a caring heart.

Practice effective communication, such as validating the emotion behind the behavior during times of distress or pain. This is important in order to build your children's self-trust to help them through the hardships they will experience as independent adults.

Encouraging self-regulation

While they are young, you have to remind your children of the need for self-regulation. You have to walk them through the process of awareness, trust, and solutions. Help them find what helps in the moment. My son, who struggles with anger, doesn't care for The Turnaround, so we've found some other options that have been helpful. I usually have to ask him, "Okay, bud. What do you need from me to help you remember to calm yourself?" (That triggers him to focus on self-awareness.) Then, I ask, "What do you want to do to feel better?" (That's the self-regulation.) I have accepted that, for him, it isn't an immediate solution; his approach is evolving and changing quicker than my other boys'. Some approaches that have been successful include:

- Hit the "reset button" (I literally just push his nose and make a robot sound)
- Return to the coping skills list
- Give a Mississippi hug
- Sing a favorite song
- Take a deep breath
- Engage tickles

A Mississippi hug is a mindful, purposeful embrace. Hugs that last 8–10 seconds have been known to release oxytocin, so a Mississippi hug helps you and your child slow down time. During your hug, you repeat this mantra out loud:

One Mississippi and two

Three Mississippi with you

Four Mississippi and five

Six Mississippi hold tight

Seven Mississippi and eight

Nine Mississippi just wait

Ten Mississippi all snug

I feel good with a Mississippi hug

Emotions are hard to regulate. Even as adults, we are still learning how to regulate our own. Our job as parents is to expect the drama and exaggeration and to teach self-regulation. The best way to accomplish this is by modeling, but they can't read our minds. Modeling may not be as obvious as we'd like. Sometimes, we need to create a narrative to coexist with the modeling. Self-regulation can help teach how to power through a tough moment (and an added plus: they might even recognize that you're a human being as well!).

For example, let's say you are experiencing a stressful moment or day. If you were unable to regulate your emotions, you could easily break down into tears or completely "lose it." But if you're able to become self-aware and self-regulate so you don't "lose it," you might model this behavior by verbally expressing something along the lines of, "Gosh, what a day! I could cry. And maybe I should, but I can't right now since we're about to walk into the store. I am going to close my eyes for a few seconds and breathe deeply. I will allow myself to cry once we get home, if I still feel this way."

An easy breathing exercise I like to do with my boys is what we call The Candle. Close your eyes, and hold your finger up to your nose. Imagine your finger is a really yummy smelling candle. Now, take a deep breath in to smell that candle. Finally, blow that candle out! Try it again and again until you feel calm.

Attunement and atonement

Because we are not perfect, we have to allow ourselves to not only become self-aware and to self-regulate but must also practice both attunement (the ability to respond appropriately to others' emotional states and behaviors) and atonement (the ability to apologize for wrongdoing). The best way to teach our children these acts is to model them in your own relationships.

Attunement is closely connected to the act of validation. However, it isn't only validation. It can look like giving a hug to your child who is crying over something that you may find silly but that clearly affects them in a real way. You don't have to say a word, just offer some physical comfort. Or perhaps you are at a family gathering and you notice your daughter breathing heavily, her eyes starting to water, so you ask her to go get you something out of the car just so she can escape and have a second to cry or breathe away from the noise. In order to give our kids some relief from the overwhelming sense of emotional confusion while they learn how to be emotionally mature, it is our job to stay attuned with how they are feeling.

This act will model to them how to do this for others, helping them to connect and empathize in future relationships.

Atonement is a challenge. Saying, "I'm sorry," is typically hard for most people, especially for teenagers, who don't want to hear the "I told you so" lectures. Some feel that saying "I'm sorry" means they have lost a battle or are admitting they are wrong. Sometimes they *are* wrong, but sometimes it's about apologizing for the inconsideration or the emotion perceived on the other end. Even when your intentions are positive, the perception of others creates the conflict. If your child can recognize the feeling that was absorbed by the other person, they'll be able to see that it isn't about who was right and who was wrong but about empathy. You model this by also freely saying "I'm sorry."

You might, for example, say something like this: "I'm so sorry that I made you feel that way. I was trying to get everything into the car quickly, and I snapped. I didn't mean to. I will try harder next time to control my tone of voice." Be careful not to ever say "I'm sorry you feel that way," but, rather, remember that your intention was simply misinterpreted. Whether they were being sensitive or you were being insensitive (or both), making a statement like that will minimize their emotions and make them feel they are not allowed to express how they feel. It is being defensive rather than open to their emotions.

Practicing atonement as the parent in the relationship will help minimize the walls between you and your child. Showing your child that you, too, are human and make mistakes will help the mutual respect remain strong. When you begin to recognize that your child or teen has emotionally matured, and they come to you with atonement, be aware of your response. Avoid any shaming or lecture in that moment:

"Thank you for apologizing. It makes me feel better knowing you have been thinking about your part in all of this, and I appreciate the recognition on your end. I love you. Let me know if you want help with anything or if you'd like to talk more."

A wonderful way to model atonement for your kids is practicing it in your relationships not only with them but also with your spouse *in front of* your kids. Many times, kids will witness little tiffs or spats between their parents, moments when the parents snap at each other or roll their eyes out of annoyance. This may be behavior the parents aren't completely proud of but that felt necessary in the moment. When kids witness fights or disagreements, it is important that they also witness the make-up part. Many parents do this in the privacy of their room or away from the kids. Parents don't have to have the full-on discussion to find solutions and figure out a deep issue; a simple hug and "I'm sorry for talking to you that way" in front of the kids will go a long way. It will show your kids the positive effects of conflict resolution, effective communication, connection, empathy, and the love between their parents and will give them security within the family system. Attunement and atonement present in the household will keep your family strong and prioritized.

Acceptance

The most important part of getting through emotional hurricanes is being able to find acceptance. The moment you reach acceptance, you feel an overwhelming sense of relief. The weight is lifted from your shoulders. Although it's the first step toward relief, it happens to also be the last phase of grief.

Grief isn't only about death: We grieve loss all the time: getting fired, failing a test. We grieve for a lost relationship after a break-up or losing a good friend over drama. We even grieve over losing relaxation time to work on the house or becoming a parent and losing sleep. It's all grief. Until we go through the process of grief to find acceptance, we won't start feeling better and feeling that relief.

Many times, we try to hop over acceptance to try to solve the problem or try to return to the way things used to be, but we keep getting pushed back, feeling more defeated over time. Whatever the issue is or the presenting problem that your child is facing, your first step is to help them find the acceptance—by allowing them to feel their feelings.

Next is for them to sit in that acceptance and experience some relief. They must know that whatever they are facing, as broken as they feel, as heavy as it's been, it is temporary. It might take time for it to pass, or they might have to do something about it, but most big problems are temporary.

In case your child is among those who consider suicide, make sure they are aware that they cannot just kill themselves to get rid of their problems. That doesn't actually get rid of anything; it just passes along all their broken hurt to those who love them—including you. Suicide only creates a stronger hurt than before.

Reassure your child that no emotion is a state of being; emotions come and go. Even if we are feeling broken or sad, we can experience other emotions breaking through that sadness. Happiness is not a land that we travel to, lock the door, and stay in forever, filled with sunshine and lollipops.

Most of the time, I hear this from clients: "I just want to be happy." Well yes, that would be wonderful and great, but it's extremely unrealistic. We can't get to happiness and just be happy from there on out. What we can do is work so happy emotions are more frequent in our lives. The bad emotions will break through from time to time, but the good emotions will be more consistent.

Finding purpose

Many times, people search for a single purpose, as if it's their soul mate. Teenagers experience big emotions wrapping their mind around this thing called life, and many times feel too exhausted to go on. Heck, adults feel this at times as well. However, teenagers are typically experiencing it for the first time. A soul-mate purpose just isn't a thing for most of us. We are meant to have multiple purposes throughout the ever-changing seasons of our lives. But if we focus on finding only one, we can easily be shot down and feel about an inch tall in this world; strong feelings of defeat take over, and we get stuck asking, "What's the effing point anyway?"

If your child feels as if they don't want to be here anymore, and they can't seem to come up with a reason to stay, then, they may ask themselves, "What's the point?" This is where we see how strong they are capable of being. They feel weak, but underneath those feelings of exhaustion and defeat, there is strength. Life is really hard when you don't feel like being strong, but you have to encourage your child to push through it and put in that extra effort to find the strength.

Finding purpose is one of the really hard parts of life. How can we show our teens what the purpose of going to school every day is? What is the point in making your parents happy when you feel like crap? You may not have easy answers to those questions, but helping your teen find a purpose will help them find their own answers.

Sometimes, our purposes are small, and, sometimes, they are big. The small ones help build toward the big ones. Going to school every day is a small, daily purpose for your child, but it feeds one of the bigger purposes: It will help your child find what their career path might look like or find a skill that they are naturally good at and didn't know about until now. They may meet someone in a class that will play a vital role in their life story. Their purpose as a teenager is to discover new interests and opinions, to find some independence as an individual but also to find their role within your family. Sometimes, their small purpose might be just to shower and brush their teeth that day. That's it. That's all they have the energy for. Other days, their purposes will go beyond that.

How to talk about purpose with your child

When I try to think of purpose, I try to think of the end goal. The end goal can be as simple as to feel happiness more often or to be a helper in this world.

One approach to speaking to your teen about their purpose would be like this: "I don't know why you were born. I don't know why you're still breathing in and out right now but what I do know is that you *were* born, and you are sitting here now. So, while it is hard, and it feels as if there's no reason, you're here. And I'm so glad you are. So, let's see if we can find a small purpose to help you understand what the point in all of this is."

Here are some questions you can pose to help get your teen thinking about purpose:

- What role do you play within each of your relationships— friendships, romantic relationships, familial relationships?

- What do you add to those other people's daily lives? Maybe your child is funny and makes others smile. Maybe your child's presence is enough to make someone else feel safe.

- Then, what can be done to contribute to that goal? What can get you closer?

This is where projects are perfect. Help your child find a new hobby or skill by encouraging them to create a project. A single project is not a huge commitment, so it's easier for them to get through it knowing it won't be their purpose every single day for the rest of their life—unless they love it, and if so, we are winning. But it will be something to look forward to: learning a new song on the ukulele—heck, learning to play the ukulele; learning how to master cookie decorating; painting by numbers; organizing your closet; learning a new skill in their sport.

Encourage your child to continue to do what they do already daily, but throw in something new. It could be reading all the classics by the end of the summer. If reading is not your child's thing, that's fine. Find something else.

One of my purposes as a teenager was to contribute to household needs (to make sure I got my weekly allowance), but I hated the act of actually doing it, so I found a way to make it bearable. My daily chore growing up was to empty the dishwasher. I'm not sure if I hated it before it became my daily chore or if it being my daily chore made me hate it, but I still hate it to this day. In order to find my way through it every single day, I challenged myself. I would put my Eggo waffles into the toaster, and I had to be done unloading the dishwasher before they popped up. It helped me get it done faster, and I was focused more on my silly challenge than on the actual horrible act of putting dishes away. And I got it done.

The teenager's guide to search for purpose

- Find who you admire. Find people who are wise and provide positive support in your life. Find those whom you can ask questions and learn from.

- Write your thoughts down. I mentioned I like to journal. So, I will always promote this, but it doesn't always have to be just a place that you express your emotions. It can be a place that you explore options, make plans, discover new thoughts. (If it makes you feel better, call it a notebook.)

- Become aware. Listen to yourself. What are you saying to yourself? What does your inner talk sound like? What fuels you? What drags you down? Where do you feel those good vibes?

It isn't just about saving the world and finding one purpose. It's about finding who you are, struggling through the crappy moments, and focusing on how to get from point A to point B without anyone getting hurt (physically or emotionally).

My self-growth philosophy

Just as you have your parenting philosophies figured out after reading this book, you should ask your child to create their own philosophy—their goals for their own life, but also what they want from you as a parent. Have your child make a list for their personal guidelines. It can become the foundation when facing tough decisions and uncomfortable moments. Have them answer questions such as these:

- "No matter what I go through, I want to make sure I always am a(n) _____ person toward others."

- "I may have some flaws, but I do know that I am a(n) _____ individual, and I like that about me."

- "I will continue to grow and learn to strengthen my desire to be a(n) _____ individual."

Feel free to share with them a list similar to what I shared with you, but give them a chance to think of it on their own. This is also fun to see how their thoughts, desires, and perspectives change throughout the years. Although my 4-year-old son may want to fill his out with "silly" now, as he continues to find himself, I'm excited to see what changes and what stays the same. What are your child's core values? What is important to them?

13

Understand the Need for Medication and Therapy

"A year ago, sitting here, there was no way I was open to trying medication. And I'm glad I didn't. But now that I've tried so many things and have talked to you once a week, I think I need more help. I can't get these thoughts out of my head, and I'm scared right now."

—18-YEAR-OLD STRUGGLING WITH DEPRESSION, ANXIETY, AND SUICIDAL THOUGHTS

Sometimes, those emotional hurricanes don't go away. Sometimes, our bubble baths just aren't enough, and we need something more. Sometimes, our child talks about how they want to die a few too many times and is not living a hard-good life but rather a hard-bad life. Sometimes, the option of medication and therapy needs to be available.

Although some people fear judgment or stigma when it comes to anything that involves mental health or therapy, I look at it as the opposite. If you or your child goes to therapy, you're actually choosing to take ownership and manage your hard life and your real emotions. That's a good thing. That's a strong thing. You care about your thoughts, your lifestyle, your emotional well-being. You're practicing emotional hygiene. It's like exercise for your mind, your emotions, and your mental health.

If you haven't experienced it, you may have no idea what therapy looks like, and the idea of sending your child or teen to therapy when you are unsure what to expect can be daunting.

Therapy is a place where someone can express their inner, private thoughts with comfort and safety. It is a place without judgment. It's similar to writing in a journal but with validation and helpful responses. Therapy is a place where vulnerability actually feels good instead of weak, where relief is overwhelming and security is provided. Therapy is a place where we are challenged as human beings so that we can be productive and make positive progress to achieve overall emotional stability and well-being. They don't teach conflict resolution in high school. We are not taught to prioritize our self-care and well-being there either.

We can have a hard-good life or a hard-bad life; it's on us to decide. We've all been dealt different hands, and we need to see what we have and learn to deal with them. As much as I hope that my kids will come to me for everything, as I'm sure you feel about your kids, we have to sit back and think about what will be best for them. There will be times that they confide in you, yes, but there will also be times that whatever hardship they are experiencing might be too uncomfortable. They may need an unbiased outlook, an impartial listener. You can't be unbiased. Therapy can be a helpful tool to do just that. In therapy, you can learn how to be the human you desire to be in this world while living your hard life.

Have you seen the movie *Jumanji*? Whether you've seen the one with Robin Williams or the one with The Rock, the story is about a game that kids and teenagers play that can literally kill them if they don't make the right decisions. Unexpected predators and "bad guys" appear, and if the players don't think and move quickly, they're goners. Many people play a game in real life that is similar every day. It is a risky game that can have some great effects, but it usually isn't fun getting there. If we aren't making the right moves or decisions, when the "bad guys" appear, it can get really bad and scary. What risky game am I talking about? Depression, anxiety, and medication.

For some lucky contestants, medication is easy and harmless. It helps exactly how it is meant to help. It takes the edge off and makes overwhelming situations and stressors much more manageable. Those who are struggling with a biological chemical imbalance of mental illness benefit greatly from medication. Even for those with a chemical imbalance, entering the game can be risky. It can be a long and exhausting journey that can be harmful in the process. If one starts an antidepressant and it is not metabolized correctly or doesn't do its job correctly of balancing the chemicals for that individual, it can actually create a bigger imbalance. Therefore, emotional stability may be nonexistent.

I am not antimedication. I am a fan of medication for those who need medication. But I am against handing over prescription drugs to young minds, labeling with a diagnosis because of one or two symptoms that sound similar, and sending them on their way. I am against encouraging this game as the only option for success. I believe addressing some of today's cultural influences will minimize the use of medications, and many families won't have to even attempt to play this risky game.

When Kinsley was 9, her mom started abusing her. Kinsley had two brothers, one older and one younger, who would witness their mom throw Kinsley around, hit her in the face, pull her hair, and scream at her until she lost her voice. At times, Kinsley would fight back. That would just fire her mom up even more. Kinsley and her brothers had no idea that this wasn't happening in other homes. Kinsley believed that whatever she did to cause her mom's intense reaction was deserved. She was being taught a dysfunctional family dynamic.

Kinsley now suffers from anxiety and depression because of her traumatic upbringing. She has made numerous suicide attempts and now practices self-harm to cope during stressful situations, even light stressors. She has become addicted to the relief and sensation that cutting herself provides. When I sit with Kinsley and listen to her describe her longing for a razor, I can't help but relate it to someone jonesing for a cigarette.

- "I can't wait to get home from school just to cut."

- "I've had a really hard week; all I want is to cut."

- "All I can think about is cutting. I know that once I do it, I'll feel so much better and won't need to do it anymore."

Kinsley is struggling daily to not self-harm. She started the "game" of medication at the age of 13, and after a year and a half of medication changes, suicide attempts, and hospitalization, she finally found her right mixture. When she is consistent with her medication, she has very little to practically no desire to self-harm. Kinsley needs medication to function and get through these tough years as a teenager. She needs medication to handle her emotions while processing the trauma she endured for so long. It has become one of her basic needs in order to survive.

Environmental versus biological

There are chemical imbalances within the brain that people are born with, usually genetic; that is a biological cause of mental illness. There are also environmental factors that can affect us, such as a hard, confusing season of our life or a traumatic event. If something traumatic happens to someone, it can affect the wiring in the brain, creating a chemical imbalance similar to those who are born with it. Likewise, hormones can have the strength to tap into our mental health.

We are all going to experience a level of depression or anxiety. I could spout out the diagnostic criteria for you or I can put it like this: You feel like shit. You look like shit. You want others to feel as shitty as you do.

A chemical imbalance within the brain is purely scientific. It makes life struggles that others handle just fine a bit harder for the sufferer. Some people just truly can't help but think certain thoughts, especially when those hormones jump in to join the depression. It's part of their natural being.

Depending on what that person wants to do for help, there is relief, such as talk therapy to process thoughts and emotions and learn how to build stronger emotional control or medication. Medication is a great tool for someone who has a chemical imbalance. And a lot of times, hormones can kick-start an imbalance that we didn't even know was there. This doesn't just apply to teenagers with hormones; adults go through hormonal rollercoasters as well. Many times, women are affected during pregnancy and after giving birth. We have to learn about our own individual situation, chemical imbalance or not, and choose to work with and grow from it.

Think of it as a cocktail. Everyone has their own recipe for a delicious cocktail with numerous ingredients. Some need to add a little bit of something to make it sweeter and less sour so it can taste just right. Others have the right mix from the get-go.

Winning the game

After multiple hospitalizations, numerous medication changes, and staying at a treatment facility for six months, Kinsley finally felt strong enough to tackle real life. With some fear and hesitation mixed with hopeful hearts, her parents agreed. They enrolled her in a new school and set her up with the best individual therapist they could find. However, Kinsley wasn't so sure. She had a hard time voicing her concerns, as she had already been through so many therapists and treatment centers. She was fearful her parents would become frustrated.

For added support and help, Kinsley joined my female adolescent group that meets biweekly. I facilitate this group with the philosophy that each teen is exhausted, hurting, confused, and seeking support and attention. I allow all topics to be brought up, and no question is off limits. It is a safe place for learning, growing, and expressing. Kinsley felt comfortable immediately because she had been through this many times before and knew how the process went, but also because she felt the safety, comfort, and acceptance the moment she walked into her first group session.

About a month into group, Kinsley asked her parents if I could become her individual therapist. Again, with hesitation, her parents obliged, and I began seeing Kinsley, one on one, for one hour every week. I learned in detail about her family history, her struggle with self-harm and all of her experiences in each hospital. Some sessions were filled with darkness, while others were motivating and hopeful.

A few months into working with her and her addiction to self-harming, she came in lower than I had ever seen her. She expressed the desire to not struggle through the pain. She felt her only way of comfort was to end her life, and I was forced to make the decision to keep her safe: hospitalization.

Kinsley was hospitalized for almost two weeks. She was mad at herself, mad at her parents, and mad at the world. But mostly, she was mad at me for sending her there. When she returned to therapy, I had to regain rapport and connection with her. It took many months to reconstruct our relationship.

After we reconnected, she made great progress: "It's been almost a year since your last hospitalization. I don't want to speak for you or too soon, but I can't help but notice the progress you've made. You haven't cut. You haven't experienced suicidal ideation. How do you think you've been able to do that? You have found strength. What are your thoughts on that?"

"I can't believe it's been a year. I've never gone this long without cutting or being hospitalized. Oh my gosh! I am so proud of myself! This is amazing! I honestly think it was self-awareness. I finally hit a point where I was able to be more in touch with my emotions and how to self-regulate them. I don't know. It's as if I just decided to find joy. I've accepted what has happened to me. I've accepted and forgiven my parents. I'm not holding on to any resentment anymore. My relationship with my parents has improved and gotten to a place I never would have seen happening. And then also I think that sometimes I'm just too busy. I got a job, met a boy, took some hard classes. I don't have time to sit around and put as much focus and energy on my depression. I think, before, there was just too much focus on it. I definitely have depression, and I'm glad I take medication for it, but why did everything have to revolve around it? And, then, you, of course. I've never had a therapist for this long. I've never felt so free to talk about my feelings and felt so safe."

Kinsley is now off to college, plans to major in psychology and become a therapist to help teenagers who struggle with depression and anxiety. While she still experiences moments of doubt, fear, defeat, depression, anxiety, and hurt, she has recognized that life is hard and has found her strength to be able to have a hard-good life rather than waste it as a hard-bad life.

A Final Note to Parents

hope that you have read my words with openness. I hope that what I have shared has helped make sense of what is going on. I hope it has helped create some ease and calmness within. My hope for you is that it provides hope. I want you to walk away from this knowing exactly what you need to do to help improve our culture and the silent epidemic of suicide and suicidal ideation among youth.

Become a model and advocate for your child. Help others see that asking for help isn't a horrible idea. The stigma is real, and it is hurting so many. The idea that asking for help equals weakness is literally killing our children. There are therapists, support groups, teachers, peers, parents, aunts, uncles, grandparents, siblings, pastors, coaches, and mentors who truly care. It's up to them and you to help and fight against the stigma. Show what help looks like. Show that asking for help actually equals strength, self-awareness, growth, and acceptance. And since acceptance is the first step toward relief, let's model acceptance, so others can have this amazing feeling of relief as well.

Help me take suicide off the table for our children. The system for parenting to prevent such a dark place for so many teens must go further than just today, beyond you and me. We need others to understand this cultural effect. We need to promote change across the board. Share everything we've discussed here with other parents, and have honest and open conversations with your children. Parents with itty bitty ones need to know this the most; they can help create a new cultural change that will affect the future.

Connect with your child consistently. Create a slower world for them so they can experience delayed gratification. Help them by allowing them to struggle and work through their own stuff but be there for support. Let them know that during the most emotionally confusing and challenging years of their life, you are there for guidance and support, not for shame and lectures but for true connection that will help set their foundation for overall well-being and independence so that, when they are ready to fly from the nest, nothing but coping skills, self-care, and strong communication skills are sitting on their table. Let's start showing them what to replace suicide with. Let's be that person they turn to and trust. No one will love them the way you do. Show them what that means.

Acknowledgments

First off, thank you to the parents who are joining me in my mission to make a change. The change needed to keep our children safe and help them grow. I can't do this alone, so I sincerely am grateful for your time and effort to not only read what I have to say but to go out and put it into action. Thank you.

Second, to my clients. My wonderful, young clients who make me feel 90-years-old on a daily basis and have taught me how to "spill the tea," why they are always "shook," what the hell a "thot" is, why they feel "salty" toward someone, and how to "go off, sis!" You each have had an impact on my parenting, my personal growth, and my motivation as a therapist. You have reminded me that my frosted glass is certainly frosty, and you've given me a unique insight into today's culture. I am grateful for each and every one of you. You've inspired me and scared the shit out of me all at once. You've been a piece of my journey that has gotten me here. Thank you. It's been hard af, no cap. Now, let's get this bread!

Next, my Joseph. I don't even know where to begin, and I don't want to fill the page with mushy, gushy stuff. Since the day I met you, you've been my biggest supporter—in ways I didn't know I needed support. You've pushed me (motivationally), you've encouraged me, you've help me build self-confidence, you've helped me become self-aware, and you have taught me how to find acceptance. Your laid-back ways have not only balanced my tense ways but have mellowed me out in all the right areas. I am grateful but, more so, proud to have you standing by my side and enjoying our lives together. I could've done this without you but—no, wait, I couldn't because we made those four awesome kiddos together. I couldn't have done this without you, honey. Thank you.

To my parents: We've certainly been through it, haven't we? Thank you, first off, for accidentally conceiving me back in 1985. You can call it a "nice surprise" all you want, Mom, but as an adult and a mother to four "nice surprises," I now understand that probably 98% of babies are probably born of an "oops!" Although most of my teenage years were spent with me angrily writing in my journal because I was grounded, yet again, I know I caused a lot of fear for you both. Thank you for choosing to take on the challenge and not give in to the easy way out (aka just giving me what I wanted). Thank you, Dad, for always validating my feelings before punishing me. It was very confusing for me, but at least, I felt that you heard and understood me. I have felt that comfort from you my whole life. Thank you both for actively trying to connect with me through those years even when, at times, I thought I didn't want to. Mom, thank you for showing me how to power through the fears us moms have, how to focus on the love we feel, and the power of being silly. Thank you for showing me what strong parents look like, what a strong marriage looks like, and what a strong therapist looks like. You both have contributed to my independence and success as an individual in the many roles that I play. Through all the disagreements, disconnect, and distance we have faced through the years, I have always known that I can call home and lean on you at any moment. That comfort and safety are irreplaceable. Thank you for giving me that.

To my second set of parents, the Stuckeys. Matt and Connie: I am so thankful you met me after my teen angst had settled a bit. You saw me with fresh eyes and in ways I didn't see myself yet. You helped me feel lovable and important from the start and helped me gain new perspectives on life. You welcomed me with the warmest of acceptance that I didn't know was possible. Just as your son taught me what support felt like, you two did the same. You both have had faith in me at times that for me seemed impossible. Thank you for being my role models and setting me up for success. Thank you for supporting me by helping take care of my little dudes while I'm off fulfilling my other purpose through work and this book. I never knew the phrase "you marry the family" could be so true. I am so thankful this is the family I got to marry and continue life with.

To my four favorite humans in the entire world, Beau, Tripp, Heath, and Jed: You have given me the biggest reason for pride. You each have taught me things about myself as I'm continuing to learn things about you. You inspire me. You motivate me. You drive me crazy, and that helps me stay balanced. Thank you for putting me in my place when I need it and helping me see different perspectives as each of you continue to grow more amazing each day. I don't have a favorite son; however, I do have favorite aspects about each of you.

Beau, thank you for being my helper. You're such an amazing big brother, and I know I lean on you to help more sometimes. Thank you for being there for me. Thank you for being so fun to talk to and to goof around with. I love our talks about dragons and dreaming about the what-ifs in the world. You have a big heart and a big mind. Thank you for sharing that with me.

Tripp, thank you for being the world's best snuggler. I love that you are always up for a hug or a snuggle no matter if you're mad at me, annoyed with your brothers, or deep into your video game. JoJo has always told me that I have the ability to bounce back—meaning I can be mad one second and then get over it the next. I think you also have an amazing ability to bounce back that helps balance out our chaotic days. Thank you for giving us that relief. Thank you for being super responsible for me too. You're a good big brother by setting examples of how to get tasks done. You are the perfect combo our family needs of responsibility and goofiness.

Heath, thank you for grabbing a spoon and spontaneously breaking out into song and dance with me. While your brothers think it can be annoying, you have become my little entertainer and social butterfly. Thank you for reminding me when it is a good time to let loose and get silly. You can always make me laugh.

Jed, my baby by 30 seconds, thank you for always putting me in my place. You have such a good memory, and you are right there to tell me when I remember something a little off. Thank you for reminding me when I am wrong and that grown-ups don't have all the answers. Thank you for being open with me about your feelings and feeling comfortable with me. And thank you for being my best little buddy who always wants to help or just be around me.

To the families who sat with me and shared their heartbreaking stories, thank you. Thank you for the time. Thank you for reliving some dark moments, and thank you for powering through the struggle and showing what true strength looks like. You are an inspiration and a big piece of some big, positive changes we are going to see soon.

My Aunt Joycie, thank you for being my first unofficial editor and always being honest with me. You have such a delicate way of telling me the truth, even if it might be hard for me to hear. Thank you for encouraging me and not allowing me to ever give up on my passions and dreams. You have always been a beautiful glimmer of positivity throughout my life and I am so very grateful for you.

To my wonderful friends: I have leaned on you. I have bounced crazy ideas off you. I have asked for your opinions and forced you to be honest. Thank you for sticking by me and patiently listening to my thoughts, theories, and fears. Marty, thank you for being my devil's advocate—for this book and for my real-life stressors. You've helped me see different perspectives and have walked alongside me through this journey. And thank you for letting me vent and express all of my frustrations, doubts, and worries throughout this entire process. I don't know if I would've made it without your push and encouragement.

Much gratitude is owed to the wonderful people who have helped this theory and vision go beyond just that and become a book. Greenleaf Book Group, thank you for taking a chance on me and for passionately walking me through this process. My editors, Lindsey, Nathan, and Stephanie, thank you for helping me organize and turn my jumbled-up words into a work of art. I am so grateful for your input and feedback. I would still feel chaotic if it wasn't for you all. Thank you.

About the Author

Tessa Stuckey is a mom on a mission. Raised by two psychologists, Tessa has a deep interest in human interaction and genuine relationships. As a therapist working with teenagers, she has decided to take on parenting from a new perspective. She provides motivation and hope for families across the nation; you can find more information or request her to speak at an event at www.tessastuckey.com.

Tessa and her husband, Joseph, live in Houston, Texas, where they are actively raising their four sons and continuing the fight against today's cultural effects.

Made in United States
Orlando, FL
14 May 2022

17856257R00109